Sixty Days to Sanity

A College Freshman's Struggle to Overcome Mental Illness

Peter D. Barnes

DEDICATION

This book is dedicated to my friends, family and people who helped me along the way when I could not help myself. Most of all to Josi who stood strong in the face of absurdity and my father whose life may have been easier if stigma did not stop him from getting the proper treatment. Finally to Damian, who inspired me late at night as I struggled to find the words that might help someone struggling to understand bipolar disorder.

CONTENTS

Chapter	Description	Page #

ACKNOWLEDGMENTS

Thanks to all my proofreaders and editors over the years…

Petra M	Suzanne S
Lori & Brian C	Nancy Crenshaw
Cody & Nicole V	Audrey Friedman Marcus
Paul & Julie B	Christine F
Greg M	Lorna H
Shari & Jay M	Christine Johnson
John & Becca S	Brandt S

PREFACE

In the fall of 1989, I was a wide-eyed teenager bound for college. Less than a month later, I was fighting my way out of a padded room. *Sixty Days to Sanity* is not a medical journal about bipolar disorder. It's simply my recollection of how a severe manic episode turned my world upside down, and how I returned to my life after a diagnosis of mental illness. The memories of this manic episode feel crystal clear, but when I recall the details it sometimes feels like the story of an entirely different person. *Sixty Days to Sanity* attempts to paint a picture for those who would like to understand bipolar disorder from the inside out.

My ultimate diagnosis was Bipolar I Disorder, Single Manic Episode Severe with Psychotic features, 296.04, *Diagnostic and Statistical Manual of Mental Disorders* (DSM-IV-TR). Bipolar disorder comes in different forms and treatment is based on individual diagnosis.

There are no cures for mental illness, only treatment. Available weapons are: proper diagnosis, research for better medicine, a patient and his/her family's willingness to accept and manage disorder, and a deeper public understanding to reduce stigma. It's my goal to help combat the stigma and confusion which so often accompanies bipolar disorder by offering firsthand insight into mania and its direct relation to clinical depression. I believe the importance of getting treatment for both mania and depression can be the difference between a great life and tragic death.

I would like to note that when I had the idea to write *Sixty Days to Sanity* I was twenty six and had no gray hairs, I am forty this year and have a few. I thought sharing my experience as the "every man bipolar guy" could help others. I've struggled for years to get this story right. I've edited and re-read the story countless times and almost force fed it to friends and family to get feedback. I've faced awkward silence but I've also received warm understanding. I realize now, the person who needed this book to understand bipolar disorder was me.

CHAPTER ONE

Leaving the Hospital

October 9, 1989

The lock buzzed as the door opened. "You're free to go," the nurse said with a smile, noticing my hesitation. "Thanks Linda," I replied, and smiled back as I stepped out of Wing 7. Walking down the hallway, I found it hard to hold back my emotions. I felt ecstatic to get out and overwhelmed with nausea from the uncertainty that faced me. The elevator door closed and I was free.

Outside, a heavy downpour muffled the sporadic sounds of car engines and slamming doors. My watch read 10:53 a.m. I was a few minutes early. I lit a cigarette, and my fingers shook from the chill in the air as I sucked down each drag. I hoped that Josi would show up soon so I could get the hell out of here. (Josi is my mom's first name—we've called her that for as long as I can remember.)

The flashing lights of an ambulance bounced silently off the ceiling of the walkway. Scratching my head, I surveyed the growing line of cars. I almost forgot that Josi had traded in the old beater for a new Chevy Cavalier last summer. A loud horn honked. I saw a hand frantically waving and knew it had to belong to her. I hastily flicked my cigarette into the ashtray, grabbed my bag, and raced through the rain.

The wiper blades slammed large amounts of water across the windshield, loud thumps marked each rotation. "You're soaked," Josi said as if it was a surprise I'd get wet running through the rain. "Yeah," I said rolling my eyes. "Oh, I'm just glad you're coming home," she sighed. Uncharacteristically, neither of us spoke for quite some time. She navigated her way across the parking lot with a heavy foot on the brake. As the hospital receded in the side mirror, my back slowly relaxed into the seat. It surprised me she hadn't made her usual comment about my smelling like a dirty ashtray. The lack of drama was a welcome relief.

The increased speed of the car made the job of the wiper blades easier. After what had to be a record breaking 15 minutes, Josi was the first to break the silence.

"You must be starving. Do you want a cheesesteak?" she said smiling.

"Sounds good to me," I replied. We merged onto the expressway.

She always said, "You must be starving" when she herself was hungry.

A flood of thoughts about my recent experiences filled my head as I stared out the window, my face pressed up against the cold glass. A familiar sign on the highway, "Bloomsburg 1 Mile," quickly passed overhead, then disappeared in the heavy rain. Questions about my future gnawed at me. Could I get a real job? What will my friends think of me? Will this medication work? Would I ever get back into college? What would the Army do? The weight of the day, my new freedom, and the mesmerizing yellow dashes of the center lane quickly lulled me to sleep.

CHAPTER TWO

The Freshman

End of August, 1989

"Come on. Let's go. You pack more stuff than your sister," Harry said from the driver's seat. I was leaving Valley Forge, a suburb of Philadelphia, and heading to Bloomsburg University, a college campus of eight thousand students in the middle of nowhere, Pennsylvania. "This is the last one," I said as I stuffed a plastic crate packed with cassette tapes and some concert-shirts into the trunk of Harry's car.

"If I drive fast, you'll be there in less than two hours," Harry said as I closed the passenger seat door.

My mom's head turned as she buckled her seatbelt. "Harry, drive slowly. There are speed traps all over the northeast extension and you can't afford a ticket." Josi claimed to know the location of every speed trap in the tri-state area.

"Don't worry Mrs. Barnes. I know all those traps."

"Harry, be careful. We'll meet you at the dorm," my sister Diane said as she and my mom drove away.

About a year ago, my cousin Keith had introduced Harry to my sister. Since they both had gone to Bloomsburg University, he thought the two would connect. He was right. Harry popped the question over the summer.

Harry lit a cigar and slid in a Rolling Stones tape as we pulled out of the cul-de-sac. My mom and sister meant well, but in this situation, having another guy around made me feel good.

The drive up the Pennsylvania Turnpike was smooth and it couldn't have been a nicer day. The sky was blue and leaves along the highway had begun to turn brilliant shades of red and yellow.

I only knew two other people who'd also be freshmen at Bloomsburg. Over the summer my twin brother Paul and I completed Army National Guard basic training at Fort Knox in Kentucky. A week after the training began, a fellow trainee named John Kelly mentioned he was headed to Bloomsburg University in the fall. Thousands of people trained on this base; it was a staggering coincidence that John and I ended up in the same twenty person platoon. This created an instant bond. Plus, I had someone to help me shut Paul up when he would brag that West Virginia University was five times the size of Bloomsburg. The other person I knew headed for Bloomsburg was Krissy Evans, a friend from high school.

Krissy was shy with a warm smile and curly red hair down to the middle of her back. You couldn't help but like her the moment you met her. Even though I only had two friends at Bloomsburg, I was happy they were John and Krissy.

"How's Paul makin' out at WVU?" Harry asked.

"He loves it. He can't stop talking about the girls. I told him it's too bad they're all related. He can't take the West Virginia humor, though. His only comeback is 'Yeah, but the Bloomsburg girls are straight off the farm.'"

"WVU does have a great football team," Harry puffed on his cigar.

"Yeah, but this year Bloomsburg has a five-to-one girl-to-guy ratio," I said proudly.

"Five-to-one?" Harry pressed his foot down on the gas pedal.

Classic movies like *Animal House* and *Fandango* shaped my image of college and now this fantasy world was a few exits away from reality. College girls, parties, no parents, and cool classes—I could hardly keep from reaching over and pressing the gas pedal myself.

As much as I wanted to party at Bloomsburg, I was equally as excited about classes. My brother and I had joined the National Guard and gone to basic training in part because my mom, being a single mom, couldn't afford to send two of us to college. I picked Bloomsburg because it was a relatively inexpensive state university that still had great educational reputation. Josi was going to try and help us financially when she could, but the G I Bill really made it possible. We both planned to get part-time jobs at school after our first semester to supplement what the army didn't cover. Since she never went to college we both wanted to make her proud.

Before I knew it a sign came into sight, *Bloomsburg 1 Mile*. On the way to the dorm, Harry honked as we drove by his old fraternity house. Two guys smoked cigarettes on the broken-down porch with kegs decorating the entrance. Up the hill parents and students walked around the main part of campus. The car stopped and I stepped out and stretched my arms high in the air. I couldn't have asked for a better place in the world.

Josi, Diane, and Harry helped me carry my crates and boxes. A man sporting a maroon and gold baseball hat with the Bloomsburg Huskies logo sat behind a fold-up table. "Welcome to Navy Hall, may I point you in the right direction?" he looked up from his papers.

"We're here with Peter Barnes. Which room is his?" Josi said with pride.

"Peter Barnes, let me see…room 205, a quick right down the hall, take a left, then about midway down the hallway."

"What a nice gentleman! Are you in charge here?"

"I'm the resident manager, but I should be called the resident babysitter," he said shaking my mom's hand.

"Josi Barnes, nice to meet you."

"Dan Crenshaw, nice to meet you, Mrs. Barnes. If you have any questions I'll be here all day."

We made our way down two narrow halls to room 205. My roommate hadn't arrived yet. My new home had plain, white concrete walls, two army-like metal beds, two desks and a small bathroom. The space was small but perfect.

"This isn't a nice view." Josi pulled back the curtains. The only window faced a brick wall of the building next door. There was a busy walkway between the two buildings. Josi turned her attention to the bare mattress.

Just then a pair of beautiful tanned legs walked in front of the window.

"What are you talking about? The view's fine by me!" Harry and Diane laughed.

I shuffled my belongings into the corners of the room. Safety pamphlets were scattered on the desks and Josi read them out loud to us. I strongly hinted for her to get on the road. "I'm not leaving this room until you have a fresh set of sheets on that mattress, end of story." Before I could protest, she was stuffing a pillow into a clean case. My sister had her own place, and with my brother in West Virginia my mother now faced returning to an empty house. My one desire was to be left on my own. Our mutual stubbornness turned into an argument.

"Listen, I can make my own freaking bed, for Christ's sake. I just finished basic training, didn't I?" I felt like I was ten years old.

I walked out and let her put on the damn sheets. I dodged parents and kids coming in and out of rooms. Jimi Hendrix and Absolut Vodka posters were everywhere. Public Enemy's "Fight the Power" blared from a room down the hall. The proud occupant had a "Vanilla Ice style" haircut. There were rules posted, a lot of rules. The top two were:

1) No ALCOHOL on CAMPUS.

2) No FEMALE VISITORS after 10:00 p.m.

This made no sense to me. Weren't drinking and women the main purpose of college? This wouldn't do. I knew I'd break those rules as fast as I could.

A short time later, we said our goodbyes. I wanted to avoid the inevitable mushy scene. "I'm excited for you," Josi wiped tears from her eyes, grabbed me in a bear hug and planted an embarrassing kiss on my cheek. You might think I'd joined the Foreign Legion, never to be seen again, when I was only two hours from home.

"Have a great semester," Harry said, patting me on the back like a coach.

"Are you sure we can't do anything else?" Diane asked and hugged me.

"I'm cool, thanks for moving all my stuff."

Diane gave me an emphatic smile. "Well, be safe, little brother." They all looked proud of me, and I felt great as they drove away, waving. Everyone was happy.

I stood awkwardly in line to register for classes with an overloaded book bag weighing down my shoulder and a list of elective courses in my hand. The girl in front of me turned around and asked flirtatiously, "So, like which classes are the easiest?" We joked about taking bowling as a major and talked about which classes we had and where we were from. She maneuvered her hand in between her books and her purse to shake and told me her name was Sherry from Cherry Hill New Jersey. Sherry was a few inches taller then me with big hair and a tan that said she spent most the summer at the beach. At a whopping five foot six, all my girlfriends to this point had been as tall or taller then me. She asked me if I knew of any parties. "I just got here a few hours ago, I'll tell you if I hear of any for sure. What dorm are you in?" I asked. "I'm in Montour Hall," she said writing her phone number on the edge of a piece of paper and tearing it off for me.

A smile came across my face and I thought life couldn't get much better. Maybe because I was in the best shape I'd ever been in from training in the Army all summer, or my new status as a college student, but I felt I could do anything. I breathed in my freedom and loved it.

Back in the dorm I introduced myself to the other guys on my wing. A few of us decided to check out the cafeteria. We were loud enough to draw dirty looks from the ladies behind the counter. We filled our trays with massive amounts of food and gawked at the opposite sex. Jerry was by far the least shy of the group. After we agreed on which table had the best looking women, he got up, strutted over like he was Tom Cruise and asked if they wanted to come hang at our dorm later. The table of red faces practically burst out laughing at his cheesy approach. "Hey, he looks kinda like Kirk Cameron from *Growing Pains*," one of the girls blurted out. It stuck; Jerry had a nickname halfway through the first day. To his credit he left the table with a phone number on a napkin.

"See, I told you it's easy. They're coming over tonight!" he bragged as his roommate congratulated him with a handshake involving several moves. His boldness was admired by everyone. I mentioned the rule about no female visitors after ten at night. A plan was quickly hatched to have the ladies enter through the window furthest from the resident manager's room. We quickly realized that even though we came from different places, we all had one noble goal: to meet as many girls as humanly possible! My college fantasies were falling into place.

Making new friends was easier than I'd imagined. We spent the afternoon checking out each other's rooms and trading music. I broke some tension with a bottle of cheap vodka I'd snuck in my bag for this occasion. It turned out most of the other guys on our dorm floor had the same idea. One by one, bottles of alcohol camouflaged in plastic soda containers somehow found their way into my room. Steve, a pale, skinny guy, who looked like he spent too much time playing *Dungeons & Dragons*, volunteered to go to the store to grab sodas and orange juice. A small party had formed. The conversation went from high school party war stories to favorite sports teams. Somebody noticed Jay, Jerry's roommate, was also a ringer for a celebrity, but no one could put their finger on who it was. I could picture the show, but couldn't remember the name. Everyone guessed.

"You know, it's the stupid show about the high school with the dorky kid Screech and the blonde guy who looks like Ricky Schroeder," I said.

Steve blurted out, *Saved by the Bell*" followed by a loud burp.

"I knew I wasn't crazy," I gave Steve a high five.

A guy who lived down the hall belted out with a laugh, "Yeah, he looks like Slater, the wrestler dude."

A chain reaction erupted, now everyone called him Slater. Jay didn't take this well. He jumped across the bed and put Steve in a headlock.

"Slater the wrestler, huh? I'll show you wrestling."

"I was just kidding, man," Steve tried to pull away.

Even though they were joking around, body parts bounced around my room.

I picked up bottles in a feeble attempt to save my room from getting trashed.

The more people drank alcohol, the louder the room was. Bets flew around the room on the chances the girls from the cafeteria would show. After midnight passed, we owned up to the fact that we'd been blown off. Slater, Steve, Kirk, and I were the last standing; we made one final toast to the first day of college and called it a night.

Everyone left and I cleaned the room, then lay in bed listening to a mixed tape on my Walkman. I didn't feel the least bit tired.

In the morning, keys jingled in the door lock. The room was blazing hot. A guy who stood about six-foot-three walked in with a stuffed duffel bag over his shoulder. My roommate introduced himself as Matt from Long Island. He had a thick New York accent like you might hear on a television crime drama. I told him about the party and about some of the guys I'd met on our dorm wing.

"Man, I'm sorry I missed out. Sounds like you had a blast," Matt said as he pulled lacrosse equipment out of the bag. We exchanged the basics about who would use which desk and on what side of the closet we'd put our clothes. I asked him about the gear and he said he was recruited to play on the Bloomsburg lacrosse team. He seemed like a genuinely nice guy and that's all I had hoped for in a roommate.

Friday night I got a call from Krissy. "Hey, Pete, I got invited to a party tomorrow night. Do you want to come?"

I was so glad to hear from her. "Sure, can I bring some friends?"

"How many?"

"I don't know—about three others?"

"I guess it'll be fine. The guy said it would be a big party; just don't bring the whole dorm." Krissy sounded a little worried.

"I promise you'll like my friends," I quickly replied.

"Meet us in the Colombia lobby at nine."

"Cool, see you there!" I hung up.

Two seconds later I was on the line with my friend John Kelly from basic training.

"Hey, Private. We have a mission," I barked.

"No shit, that's great. Where's the party?"

I gave him the details and he seemed excited. This would be the first time we'd hung out outside of the army. I continued to spread the word around my floor.

Friday night, Steve, Kirk, Slater, John, and I followed the ladies to the party like puppies. I wore a blue and white absolute vodka t-shirt, tan shorts, checkered Vans sneakers and my hat backwards.

Krissy's friend asked who smelled like cologne? I fessed up that it was me. I had put on some Obsession that my girlfriend in high school gave me as a birthday present a year before.

Music blared from a row of student apartments up the hill. As it got louder, our footsteps quickened. This was the last weekend before classes began and the whole campus was out. The Beastie Boy's "Brass Monkey" thumped on a bad sound system when we walked into a crowded, sweaty room. The smell of stale beer engulfed the senses. I thanked Krissy again for taking us with her. Without the girls there was no chance we'd have been allowed in.

I separated from the pack and made my way through the crowded room. A seat opened up at a table full of upper classmen and I sat down and joined a game of *Asshole*, already in full swing. I was familiar with the drinking game in which a hand of cards is ranked from highest to lowest: president, vice-president, secretary, and asshole. After one round, I became president. I had the power to tell anyone ranked below me to drink at any time. I felt unstoppable. When the game broke up, John nudged me to go to the hallway and I followed.

"So, what's the story with Krissy? Are you dating or something?"

"No. We've been friends forever. Why?"

"It's no big deal, she's nice," John took a sip from his plastic cup.

"Nice?" I knew exactly what he was getting at.

"What? Okay, she's nice and cute."

"You know the best thing about Krissy?" I paused and made sure she wasn't eavesdropping, then continued. "Remember in basic training when I told you about my friend Brian, the one who has Cerebral Palsy?

"Yeah?" John said puzzled.

"When Krissy heard he was having trouble finding a date to the prom, she asked him to go with her."

"No shit, that's cool," John said.

"I don't know if she would go for a guy like you, but I'll put in a good word for ya," I said as we walked back into the main room.

In the kitchen, a girl, who at this point in the night looked like Brooke Shields, handed me a bottle of "Mad Dog 20/20." The sour taste was nasty, but I drank it anyway. The party began to break up. John, Krissy, and most of the people we came with made their way back to campus. I was having way too much fun and decided to stay. I found myself rambling on to the girl who had handed me the bottle about my position as hooker on my high school rugby team. I was amazed she didn't walk away. Instead she put her hand on the counter next to me and came a little closer.

"You're funny," she said playfully.

"I'll take funny." I said awkwardly, a bit caught off guard by the fact a sophomore might be into me.

Her hair was dark brown; she wore a white button-down shirt, a powder-blue skirt, and sneakers without socks. Her name was Nikki, or at least that's what I think she said. She was visibly drunker than I was. We stood by the rail of the deck looking over campus. After a minute of small talk, we were locked in a sloppy drunk kiss.

When we came up for air, she pulled me by the arm, "Come on, let's go."

"Where are we going?" I asked, as if it mattered.

We wound up hopping from party to party. She knew everyone and kept introducing me as "this cute freshman I picked up." I felt no pain, I was ready for anything. At one of the last parties, we found my dorm mate, Jerry a.k.a. "Kirk." I was so glad to see someone I knew; he was my proof I ended up with a sophomore.

Nikki used my arm as her sole means of balance as we walked down the street. Enjoying the warm night, we walked to the steps of the main campus building, Carver Hall—a typical college centerpiece with a massive, white dome. The stairs were well lit and made it seem like daylight, but it had to be after three in the morning.

I flinched as Nikki took my hat off and ran her fingers over my hair which had been shaved off at the beginning of the summer during Army training.

"Ahh, let me, it's so fuzzy, I love the way it feels," Nikki slurred as we made it to the top step.

Who was I to argue? I hadn't even kissed a girl since before the summer started.

"So what are your friends like back home?" Nikki asked.

"Let's see. I have a twin brother."

She pushed me. "No way, there are two of you?"

"We're fraternal—we don't look alike," I said.

"Who's better looking?" Nikki moved closer.

"You'd have to figure that out for yourself."

"Does he have a nice smile and adorable freckles like you?" She smiled putting her hand on my face.

"That's funny. No, as a matter of fact, people say he looks like my dad and I look like my grandfather." I said.

"Was he at the party?" she asked.

I explained that Paul and about five of our friends had all picked West Virginia for its reputation as a party school.

"Why'd you pick Bloomsburg? It's so lame." she lit a cigarette.

"It's not bad so far. Plus it's the only college I applied to. I visited my sister in her senior year—I was 16 then and had so much fun, I knew this was the place for me." I took a drag of her smoke.

"By next year you'll be bored out of your mind; you see the same people over and over," Nikki said with a sigh.

Her skirt crept up her thigh. I had an incredibly hard time concentrating on anything she said. I put my arm around her shoulder and tried to regain my composure. My brother will be so jealous when I tell him about this, I thought to myself.

The next thing I knew, we were tangled up kissing. I didn't care who saw us, this was the kind of night I'd dreamed of.

We stopped every ten feet to kiss and grope each other as we made our way back to her place. She lived in an apartment above a bakery, and shared it with two other people. A guy wearing a Grateful Dead T-shirt was asleep on the couch. A bong sat on the table next to an overloaded ashtray and beer cans were scattered around.

"I have to use the lady's room. Hang out for a second." Nikki disappeared into a hallway. I looked at a clock and it was almost four in the morning. I noticed that even though I had been drinking all night, I wasn't the slightest bit tired. Unaware of any change, I simply felt great, as I explored my new world.

The living room was illuminated by the harsh glow of an infomercial on the television. The sound was off, yet the amazing cooking device sucked me in. Before I could turn up the volume to find out how I could purchase the wonderful invention, Nikki grabbed my wrist and pulled me into her bedroom.

In contrast to the disheveled living room, her room was clean and smelled fantastic. A futon mattress on the floor was covered with a plaid comforter. Scented candles had been lit and Depeche Mode played on her stereo. Framed pictures of cute girlfriends holding drinks in the air were neatly placed on her shelves. A collage with corny sayings clipped from magazines hung next to a trippy poster, with a clock melting in the branches of tree. Before I could comment on her décor, she wrapped her arms around me.

As we kissed again, I stopped. "I didn't bring any condoms." I said, kicking myself for leaving them back at the dorm.

"You're a cocky little one aren't you? Besides, I'm on the pill, silly."

"I didn't mean it like that." I backpedaled.

"Don't worry Peetttyyy, let's just see what happens." she whispered. I had a sneaking suspicion she'd done this before.

My energy was boundless that night. I didn't want to stop touching and kissing Nikki. After our alcohol-induced passion subsided, she put her head on my chest and closed her eyes. I couldn't sleep. I blathered on about my grand plans for life, how beautiful she was, how life was so spectacular. I felt like Charlie from *Willy Wonka & the Chocolate Factory* the moment he discovered his golden ticket. As the morning sun blazed through the crack in the curtain, she realized I was never going to shut up. Tired and annoyed, she abruptly rolled to the other side of the bed.

I kissed her between her shoulder blades hoping to get her turned on again.

Suddenly, pissed off, she looked at me and said, "What's wrong with you? Are you ever going to shut up and go to bed?"

"I'm sorry, just wanted to kiss you," I pulled back.

"Listen, I gotta sleep. You're gonna have to leave now."

The fact that she was upset did not compute. "What's your number? I'll call you later."

"I don't have a phone. Listen, just let me sleep, she said, burying her face back into the pillow."

I practically skipped back to my room. All I needed was some rain and an umbrella to complete the scene.

The second I got to my room, I woke Matt my roommate up and told him about my night. Surprisingly he didn't kick my ass for waking him up at six in the morning. He was short on stories at this point, so he thought my antics were hilarious. He must have had the patience of Job. Whether he believed me or not, I may never know.

Unaware, he'd drifted back to sleep, I continued on about the night's tales.

Staring at the ceiling, hands behind my head, I debated. The rational part of my mind told me to sleep, but the pedal controlling my energy level pressed towards the floor.

As I lay motionless, a sensation I'd never felt before ran through my entire body. I could only attempt to describe the feeling as a gentle tickle. Suddenly I began to rise, traveling like a balloon that had barely enough helium to keep floating. I thought it might be a dream but it wasn't like any dream I'd ever had. When I reached the ceiling I could see the entire room, including myself in the bed below. Matt's lacrosse helmet, stick, and shoulder pads were scattered in the corner. The concrete blocks felt cold on my fingertips, as I pushed off the wall, propelling my second-self around the room. Matt looked funny in his boxer shorts, white socks, and pale legs. Sweat poured from his forehead as if he'd been exercising. After a minute of floating around the room, I fell, and effortlessly merged back into my body on the bed.

Unable to comprehend this experience, I continued to lie still, with a smile plastered on my face. Thoughts of euphoria filled my head. I was becoming a fucking superhero for Christ's sake! Then, I had a brilliant revelation. I unlocked an incredible secret hidden deep inside my brain, information powerful enough to double the productivity of the human race. For the first time, I realized sleep was a primitive invention of our ancestors, who must have been extremely lazy. My mission: let the planet know that sleep wasn't necessary.

A knock on the door broke me out of my hypnotic state. I opened the door and Matt began to stir. Matt introduced me to Frank, his best friend and high school lacrosse teammate, who lived in another dorm across campus. Frank's accent was thicker than Matt's. He tried to get Matt up for breakfast. Before Matt had a chance to even get up out of bed, I told them my new theory, sleep was bogus. Frank and Matt thought I was still drunk from the night before. We went to breakfast together and I couldn't stop talking. When we went back to the dorm, Matt went back to sleep.

I couldn't sit in our room anymore. I needed to find people moving at a faster pace. My head swelled with ideas. I thought, I've got to let the public know what they're missing. I was convinced the whole world would be more productive and fun if nobody had to sleep. At least I'd have more people to hang out with.

My mind was like a stationary exercise bike, pedals spinning at light-speed, but moving nowhere. The fear button in my head had been disabled and the obnoxious level cranked high. It took me about ten minutes in an art history lecture hall to realize I was a hundred times smarter than the professors. I decided my time would be better served learning on my own, outside the classroom. Ads in the weekly school newspaper listed clubs looking for new members. This sounded fascinating! I wanted to join every one, and that's what I set out to do. I started with the student government meeting, then the school newspaper. I spent all my time going from group to group. I had pieces of papers explaining club dues, history and anything else they could throw at me. I was told joining these clubs would help my resume, but I neglected to see that going to classes might help with the resume, too.

The paper said the first rugby meeting met that night. I strutted into the meeting as if I were coach of the Olympic team. In my mind, having played rugby for three years in high school made me a leading expert in the sport. The person running the meeting was a monster of a guy who looked to be about 250 pounds. He asked if anyone had any questions. I listened patiently to another guy for about ten seconds and then began to take over. I eagerly stood up and laid out my idea to make Bloomsburg the best rugby club ever. Thirty college rugby players sat and listened to a hundred and thirty pound motor mouth freshman tell them how to run their club.

My plan included an idea for "Rugger Huggers." I'd seen the phrase on a bumper sticker somewhere. Rugger Huggers were to be our fan club and cheerleaders all in one. The next day, I frantically made over 100 posters with obscene sayings on them like, "Support your rugby team, give head" and "Bring a great attitude and a great pair of tits." I held up the line for the copier trying to make the posters just right. I plastered them everywhere without permission from the club or university officials. Taping them to the windows of a female dorm got me nabbed. The less-than-supportive campus police didn't take kindly to my works of art that would have made Hunter S. Thompson proud. They grabbed me by the arm as I put one up. I turned and said, "What the hell?" Two security guards with freshly starched uniforms and serious attitudes stood behind me. The older of the two told me to hand over the rest of the signs. The other threatened me by saying the rugby team would lose their field because of me. At this point, I felt like Rosa Parks at the back of the bus. I began to argue the First Amendment. It didn't work. I didn't see anything wrong with the posters. They made me take down every one. The team members were not happy about possibly losing the field. Some girls were offended by the posters, but a lot more thought the slogans were funny. At the next meeting, more than 30 girls signed up to become Rugger Huggers. Once the threat of losing the field was gone, I was out of the shithouse and immediately chosen as the new social director of the club.

I no longer had any time for my friends John and Krissy. I was consumed with plans to enlighten the world with my new ideas, or at least Bloomsburg for the moment.

Days went by and I felt super-energized. This no-sleep thing was incredible! Underlying this elation was the constant feeling of never being satisfied. I wanted to walk faster, talk faster, eat more, touch more, laugh more....No one seemed able to keep up with me. I felt superior but didn't exactly know why. Talking with people around campus felt like talking to children. Yet I desperately wanted them to acknowledge my brilliance. I made my way from one conversation to another like a clown moving around a child's party. I stopped to talk with anyone who dared make eye contact. Humor was how I chose to communicate my message, but I needed a larger forum to reach everyone at once. As I flipped through the student newspaper again, the answer jumped out. *WBUQ Bloomsburg's Campus Radio Station Meeting Tonight, DJ's Needed for All Shifts.* With the same energy and forthrightness as I had entered the rugby meeting, I headed for the college radio station.

I strolled in late as people took their seats. Sitting in the back row I cracked jokes to anyone who'd listen. A pudgy Asian girl dressed entirely in black with the exception of red and white stripped knee socks sat at the desk next to me. She didn't have any sense of humor. Instead of laughing, she simply clutched to her chest a three-ring binder with a hand drawn picture of Morrissey on the cover and came just short of sticking her tongue out at me. A tall thin guy wearing glasses and week-old facial scruff stood up and introduced himself as general manager of the station. I hurriedly finished telling the girl next to me how I would put WBUQ on the map within a week. The station manager shot me a nasty look but continued to explain how the schedule worked and what show formats needed to be filled. I leaped up and said, "Are you all ready for the greatest radio show this campus has ever heard?" Everyone in the room looked at me like I was a three-headed rattlesnake. He looked over at the girl I'd been talking to as if to ask her if she knew me. She shrugged her shoulders.

"Sorry buddy, we don't have a slot for that show this semester," he said, and everyone laughed.

"What the hell do you know? You're a fucking dork." I said angrily.

The room turned silent.

"This lame amateur two-bit college station wouldn't know a cool show if it smacked you in the face!" I yelled, storming out of the room.

My mood turned a hundred and eighty degrees in seconds. These simpletons couldn't understand my genius.

Halfway down I turned around and I ran back to the door and screamed, "You guys are all losers if you sit here and listen to this idiot! Ha!" Then I ran out of the building laughing to myself. When I got across campus, I had to stop and catch my breath. I was definitely not welcomed back.

Without hesitation I headed for WHLM, the local rock station. I hadn't heard the station, but I'd seen a sign on a downtown building earlier in the week. I figured professionals would get me. I opened the back door and went up a narrow flight of stairs. There was a black door at the top of the stairs with a sign, WHLM. Bingo! I'd hit the jackpot. A small, red "On Air" light glowed above the door. I waited until it went dark then knocked. A lady opened the door with a cigarette in her hand. She wore a flannel shirt tucked into designer jeans that were a size too small.

"Can I help you? Don't tell me you lost your dog," she said blowing smoke up into the air.

"No, not exactly," I replied, grinning ear to ear.

"Then what can I do ya for? I've got to be on air in a minute," she walked back towards the studio.

I followed close behind, I wanted to see a DJ talking over the air. After reading the weather and local news, she took the headphones off and came back to hear me out. I explained why I'd be perfect for the overnight shift, describing how my show would change the world.

"You see, I found out the other day that human beings actually don't need sleep. It's totally unnecessary."

"Oh really?" She said sarcastically, now on her third cigarette.

I knew I had the job. Or at least that's what I thought. In reality, she may have told me I could someday become a DJ or something else to make me feel good. I walked out the door, patting myself on the back. I couldn't wait to start. In my mind I was already a WHLM employee.

Walking back down the stairs, I thought of a great publicity stunt for my show and I went back to tell her the good news. To my surprise, the door was locked. She must have locked the door the second I left. Puzzled, I banged on the door. I tried to open it a few times, then decided I couldn't waste any more time. I'd tell her later I thought, going on my merry way.

From a few blocks away, I looked back and saw a cop car pulling up to the station. I paused for a second to admire the flashing lights. I never suspected they were meant for me.

CHAPTER THREE

Day Seven: Sleep is for Fools

September 7, 1989

At this point I hadn't slept for five days. The longer I stayed up, the more powerful I became. Every night of the week a party happened somewhere. I drank beer, smoked pot, and did shots with drunks. I latched onto any girl willing to listen to me. After everyone went to sleep I took long walks while listening to my Walkman and thinking about the universe. I always brought a notebook to make sure I captured my great ideas on paper. My thoughts would flow faster than I could write, much to my frustration. As soon as I got a good one, I wanted to act on it. A strong belief that telepathic communication would rule the future reoccurred over and over. I tried to read the minds of passersby. I knew it would take time to master the art of telepathy, but I was prepared for the long haul.

Once I started talking to someone, I couldn't help but relate all these revelations. I just had to get it out. Being the only one up all the time started to get lonely. Life would be more fun when everyone finally accepted the obvious. As the "World's Greatest DJ," I'd soon get my message out on a massive scale. The world would be so productive, we were on the brink of a revolution that would change the planet in fantastic ways. People would dance in the streets when I exposed the true power of the mind.

As the morning sun began to rise over the hills, I sat on the steps of my dorm, wallowing in delight thinking of how intelligent I'd become. College felt like grade school to me. I realized all of my high school teachers lied about how hard college was to keep us coming to class. Since classes were so easy I figured it would be best if I just read the books necessary to graduate on my own. In doing so I could finish in a year and move on to my doctorate.

I went to the bookstore and waited for it to open. When it did, I stuffed my book bag with as many books as possible. I planned on reading until I finished every book. Walking to the library, I found my spot in the corner section on the second floor. The aisles of books in every direction were protecting me on my critical mission. With all of this material surrounding me, it felt like I could suck knowledge out of the air through osmosis.

The previous year, I'd watched an infomercial about speed-reading. At the time, I didn't believe in it, but now it made perfect sense. I practiced the techniques I remembered from the show--my reading speed grew exponentially. I polished off a seven hundred page economics book in an hour. I had the power to absorb information at an inhuman rate. I didn't leave my chair except to use the bathroom.

My cerebral hemispheres swelled like Arnold Schwarzenegger's biceps. Feverishly I marked pages, highlighted sections, wrote notes. I laughed out loud to myself when the "ah ha" effect came to me. "Excuse me, the library closes in five minutes," an older lady said in a meek voice.

"No problem," I replied. It was midnight.

I moved my portable think tank outside, under the bright lights of one of the gigantic brick buildings. The night was beautiful and calm. I could hear the periodic "tttzzzzzz" of innocent insects being exterminated by a nearby bug-zapper. I kept reading. At this rate, I'd graduate in no time.

Around four in the morning, I decided to take a break from the books and walk in no particular direction. I pulled out my Walkman and popped in a tape my high school girlfriend gave me the day we broke up. *Black Coffee in Bed* by Squeeze played and I couldn't help but think of Tara.

Until senior year, Tara and I hadn't seen each other since we'd both changed schools in the fourth grade. We reconnected at a mutual friend's party; after a few minutes, we talked like old friends. I fell hard. She was athletic, had shoulder-length black hair and the most adorable Irish freckles. Tara wasn't the first girl you'd notice at a party, but she's the one you'd want to get to know by the end of the night.

Our senior year we were with each other all the time. Tara came to all my rugby games, in turn I went to all her lacrosse games, and we both got two proms out of the deal. In the month before graduation we talked and both agreed we didn't want to get 'serious.' A few days before Paul and I left for basic training our friends went to the Jersey Shore for the weekend. We took a stroll on the beach. This was the final breakup talk.

"I don't know how to say this without sounding like a bitch," she said pulling back a little.

I knew what came next.

"We've had such a great time," she looked down. "We aren't even gonna be at the same college next year, I just don't see the point," Tara said bluntly.

"I know, I know," I said, kicking the sand.

If I weren't leaving for basic training, I might be saying the same thing to her. But I'd definitely miss her.

"I promise I'll write if you send me your address. I made this tape, it's all the songs we like," she said, handing me a cassette tape, with, P&K's senior year favorites written on the cover. "You made me a breakup tape." I laughed. Then she wrapped her arms around me for one last kiss.

I wondered what Tara will say when she realizes she'd broken up with the most brilliant person on the planet.

Memory lane was interrupted, when my battery power died and the song sounded like it played underwater. I kept walking, through backyards and over some train tracks. I found myself on the far west end of town. Spotting a 7-11, I made my way past a disheveled old man sitting next to the doorway with an empty bottle of whiskey in his hand. The bright florescent lights of the store made me wince. I found the batteries I needed and brought them to the counter and asked for a pack of Camel Lights.

"Late night studying?" questioned a heavy-set woman behind the counter.

"Studying is for mortals, I'm the 'World's Greatest DJ!'" I said with pride.

"Oh, y'all are gonna be a DJ. How nice. What station?" she asked as her man-like fingers reached to hand me my change.

"WHLM. Do you listen to it?" I asked excitedly.

"Na, I only listen to country music," she said, walking into the back room.

The man on the sidewalk asked if I had any change. I handed him the forty-five cents change in my hand and a cigarette after I opened the new pack. I smoked, as I continued to walk away from town. Not far from the 7-11, a glow from bright lights lit the sky like a football stadium, a gigantic metal structure arched over a dirt road and led into some kind of a park. A sign at the top of the arch read *Welcome to the Bloomsburg Fairgrounds*. I didn't know if I was allowed in, but this late at night, who'd care?

The fairgrounds were big enough to hold a neighborhood of houses. The smell of horseshit was intense. Rows of vendor booths for selling cotton candy and games lined the fence. I walked across the main area that had metal bleachers twice the size of any high school football stadium. You could almost hear the tractor-pull announcer introducing the monster truck Big Foot. "Raaaaaaaaaacccccccccceeeeeeeee Fannnnsssss, Let'ssssss Gettttt Readyyyyyy to Rummmmmmbleeeeee!!!!" This was awesome!

I sat down in the middle of the arena and turned my Walkman off so I could concentrate on creating my radio show. I smoked another cigarette and looked over at a huge drilling machine. It hit me like a lightning bolt. The idea simple, and perfect! I couldn't believe something so incredible hadn't come to me sooner.

I had discovered an ingenious solution that would ultimately eliminate the need for radio stations altogether. Earlier I'd read all about the pressures and temperatures of the earth's core. My new brainchild involved constructing a transmitter strong enough to broadcast from the center of the earth. I could simply transmit my radio show telepathically to the box, and then the box could relay my message to every person on the planet. Having the box located at the center of the earth would allow the signal to transmit at equidistance to all humans without wires. We could tear down all the hideous radio towers along the highway. People would be able to trash their archaic devices--Walkmans, televisions and stereos. They would only need brain waves to receive all the news and entertainment around the globe. This would revolutionize all communications on earth. I'd be the maestro conducting the symphony. My show, of course, would be the focus but I'd open up the channels so any person could broadcast through the transmission box. Telepathic communication would catch on faster then cable TV. I needed to find an engineer to translate my brilliant thoughts--someone who could understand the dynamics of building such a box. Certainly the CIA would drill the hole, if I let them use the transmitter. I'd have to incorporate a translator application, so all languages could understand the show. My idea was possibly the answer for world peace. A chill went down my spine, with the realization of the true magnitude of what I'd discovered. This was as good as $E = mc^2$ or even Edison's light bulb! With a few large stones, I marked the spot where I thought the digging should begin.

"Don't worry world, I'm coming!" I belted at the top of my lungs and headed back towards campus to find an engineer.

Immediately I thought of Steve, the skinny guy from my dorm wing. In the past few days I'd sat in Steve's room for hours spewing out all of my amazing revelations. I was confident he had the technical savvy to help me build a transmitter box sturdy enough to withstand molten lava.

I practically fell through the door, as I turned the corner into Steve's room. Steve sat with his back to me playing a computer video game. Just as I began to unveil my plans telepathically, to ensure no one could overhear our conversation, I spotted an odd figure in the corner of his room. A puppet, a Ronald Reagan puppet, to be exact. I was impressed by the likeness to the ex-president. The arms, which had boxing gloves for hands punched when you moved the levers on its back. I felt like a child with a shiny new toy.

"Steve, whose puppet? It's gotta be the coolest thing ever." I asked out loud, the old-fashioned way.

He turned his head away from the computer game. "My little brother left it here when I moved in, don't wreck it."

Steve didn't want to part with the puppet. Then I showed him my ability to transform the lifeless doll into the aging world leader, making it impossible for him deny the obvious connection. It came as a surprise to me, I was able to talk exactly like President Regan, with the puppet attached to my arm.

"Promise you'll bring it back?" Steve asked, grudgingly.

"Well, how about I give ya some jelly beans and we call it even," I said. Doing my best Regan voice.

"I'm serious. I'll have to buy him a new one, if something happens to it," Steve whined, turning back to his computer screen.

Although becoming the "Worlds Greatest DJ" still took top priority, the puppet took over my immediate focus. I was ecstatic, as if I sat in front of a slot machine: bing, bing, bing, three Ronald Reagan puppets in a row! Another winner!

My next step was to take the puppet on the road. From then on it never left my side. As soon as I put the damn puppet on my hand, I became Ronald Reagan. To get someone's attention, all I had to do was give them a jab with the arms. This was a creative way to deliver my revolutionary messages to the general public. I was sure they would swallow it up.

The highlight of the afternoon was when I made my way to the Commons and got the attention of a real live audience. The Commons was Bloomsburg's miniature version of Central Park, a sea of gray and maroon Greek symbols. Some people sunbathed in the grassy area, others studied on benches. A dog chased a Frisbee in the far corner of the lawn. It looked fun but my time for playing games had passed. I needed to take action. I decided a nearby cluster of hacky-sackers would be the perfect test audience for my show. As smooth as humanly possible with a Ronald Reagan Punching Doll attached to my arm, I snuck towards the hack circle. I dodged a bare foot and grabbed the hack in mid-air. Then I bolted to take my position at the top of the stairs leading to the cafeteria. Now I had people's attention, I quickly tossed the hacky sack back to a guy with dreadlocks spilling out of his Rastafarian hat. A group slowly formed as I began to talk through the puppet to spread my no-sleep theory. I was in heaven.

"Mrs. Gorbachov, tear off that bra!" I said to a girl in the crowd, mocking the president's call to get the Russian leader to help tear down the Berlin Wall. I thought I was hysterical.

After every punch line, I made the punching arms go back and forth like a boxer. I was on fire. I stayed focused when I explained the benefits of not sleeping. I expounded on the power of a universe soon to be connected to a single communication source. Having a crowd was magnificent. Some people laughed hysterically, others reacted in anger at what they could not understand. I knew the ones who walked away would kick themselves once the transmitter box was up and running.

My campus routine was hot; why not take it to the next level--downtown? That night all thoughts of partying were sidetracked. My need for an audience took me to Hess Tavern, one of three bars, a hotel, and a pizza place comprising Bloomsburg's downtown. The practice from earlier in the day had me fired up and ready. I walked into Hess's, and found a mix of local rednecks and drunken college kids--the perfect crowd for a puppet show.

I explained to the bartender how I could liven up the scene; I talked so fast I confused him. He didn't even card me. A few older men around the bar gave me funny looks, but there were enough people in the room for me to make a splash. It must have been a pretty good show because when they escorted me out. I didn't have any bumps or bruises.

Nothing could stop me from spreading my ideas to the public. Next, I strolled into Sal's Pizza, the local late-night hangout. During the day the place sat empty, but at night this place was standing room only. Guns-N-Roses' *Sweet Child O' Mine* played on the jukebox. Two kids were taking turns at a Punch Out video game in the corner. It didn't take long to draw attention to myself.

I happened to catch a look from a fraternity guy sitting at a table with about five of his brothers. He looked like he'd used a whole can of mousse to get his hair to slick back. The guys wore red and black sweatshirts with the letters ΓΕΟ. Two girls who were definitely drunk were also at the table. One had a jacket with the same colors and letters. I got right in their faces with the puppet. Laughing with a piece of pizza falling halfway out of his mouth, one of the guys at the table elbowed his girlfriend and said, "He's the weirdo I told you about, the one at the Commons today."

"Are you calling the President of the United States a weirdo?" I jabbed him in the shoulder with the puppet arm.

"Check it out. He called you out with the puppet," another guy at the table said, reaching up to give the puppet hand a high five. The whole table burst out laughing.

The one who called me weirdo turned red and said, "Hey, geek, take your faggot puppet back to the dorms."

"Got it dude, like for sure," I joked back. I walked away and made rounds from table to table looking for a more receptive audience. Less then five minutes later the frat dudes and their babes got up to leave; I followed. It bothered me that they didn't understand my message.

I followed at a close distance until we reached their house. A large wooden sign hung above the front part of the porch that matched the letters on the sweatshirts they wore. House-party music thumped from inside spilling into the residential neighborhood. The one with the slicked-back hair noticed me. Adrenaline surged through my body at a fantastic rate--I knew tensions were getting high, but I didn't care.

"Look at the freak show with the puppet behind us," he pointed to me.

The front porch began to fill with people from the party coming outside to see me. I still had the puppet in my hand, as I stood in the middle of the street trying to figure out how to win over this crowd.

"Hey puppet man, come up here so we can kick your ass!" someone yelled from the porch.

"Yeah asshole, I'll show you where to stick your puppet," another idiot's voice belted out.

"I'm going inside, this is ridiculous," a girl said as she slammed the screen door.

Standing alone in the middle of a dark street with a puppet, and picking a fight with an entire fraternity didn't strike me as odd.

"You guys have no idea about the revolution coming and you're gonna miss it!" I yelled laughing, knowing I could simply tune them out when the transmitter box was complete.

Suddenly Mr. Slick Hair ran into the street towards me. About five other guys weren't far behind. I was ready for anything. As pissed off as I was for their lack of understanding, I tried until the last second to change their minds. The first guy took a shot at grabbing the puppet out of my hand. We wrestled to the ground. The puppet went flying in the commotion. After we stretched each other's shirts and got in a few punches, we both made it back to our feet. It resembled a bad scene from *Cops* as his buddies tried to hold me back. No one could restrain me. As they came at me, I started punching, kicking, and throwing people away. It wasn't pretty, but I couldn't lose the puppet.

"Just give me the puppet!" I screamed wildly.

I felt a hot sting, as a punch connected to my cheekbone. It almost knocked me down, but I recovered, completely enraged. Several arms were grabbing at me. I kicked a kneecap; then connected solidly with a face. I saw the person I hit fall over the edge of the sidewalk and heard him yelp in pain. I felt unstoppable. About fifteen feet away a guy held up the puppet yelling, "I got the stupid puppet, you freak!"

I was about to go after the puppet when the slick haired guy came at me for the second time. I've never felt so angry in my life. I caught him by his throat and ran pushing him across the street towards a parked car. My eyes were bursting with fury. We sped across the concrete. A streetlight caught the rapidly unfolding madness. My hand right hand gripped my adversary's neck, as he backpedaled until slamming into the car. His head whipped back and made a loud noise as it hit the hood. I held his collar screaming as fierce as a drill sergeant, "You fucking asshole! You have no idea who I am! What did I ever do to you? Just get him to give me the fucking puppet!" my voice trembled on the verge of tears as I screamed. The awestruck crowd gathered on the porch looked on, not knowing what would happen next.

"Give him the stupid puppet, he's not right," a girl's voice screeched from the porch.

The puppet flew up in the air before coming to rest twenty feet down the street. I let the frat boy go and turned to run for the puppet.

"You're a fucking psycho," he yelled from the safety of the porch.

The crowd dispersed and I scraped the puppet's remains off the ground.

I couldn't believe what had happened. My emotions overwhelmed me, my eyes felt swollen, as tears welled up. I wasn't sad, I was angry and confused. Tears acted as a release valve, letting the excess energy pour out like water from a broken fire hydrant. These tears actually hurt. I had never felt such powerful emotions before. My feelings of invincibility and righteousness were battling my sense of loneliness and people's lack of understanding. But the wave of insecurity didn't last long. The release of the tears had somehow cleared any insecure thoughts out of my head. By the time I'd walked a few blocks away, I was back to conquering the world.

CHAPTER FOUR

Day Fifteen: Good Morning Fort Indiantown Gap

September 15, 1989

The day after my puppet incident, I was scheduled to attend my first Army National Guard weekend since basic training. I was excited to have a fresh group of people to share my discoveries. I didn't have a car, so I had to take the bus. I stuffed all the gear I needed into a duffel bag. The phone rang; my buddy John Kelly was on the line.

"Hey, Pete, how's it going?" he said with concern.

"Things are amazing. I have so much stuff to tell you," I said excitedly.

"Yeah, I saw Krissy at breakfast. She heard you were doing some kind of puppet show at the Commons yesterday?" he said in a half question, half statement.

"Yeah, that's part of what I have to tell you. This has been the best week of my life. I don't know where to start," I poured out, almost losing my breath.

"Excited about what--did you get laid or something?"

"Yeah, but it doesn't have anything to do with what I'm talking about."

"You lucky bastard. Was it the girl from the party?"

"I'm not talking about getting laid," I said with frustration. "John, I have a drill weekend and I'm trying to catch a bus. But when I get back, I'll tell you everything. I mean everything. It's huge, believe me. You're going to get laid just because you know me," I said, smiling and looking in the mirror to see if any hair had grown back.

"Sounds good to me, call me as soon as you get back. I can't wait to hear about the girl. I still don't understand about the puppet, but if it helped you get laid. . . ." John said, a bit puzzled.

"Don't worry, it'll make perfect sense when I explain everything. When you know what I know, you'll be able to do anything you want--you can be a rock star, whatever you want," I said, still frantically packing my bag at the same time.

"If you say so. Hey, tell Paul I said 'hi' if you talk to him,"

"Shit! You reminded me, I have to call Paul before I go, talk to you later!" I hung up abruptly. I scoured my desk and found my brother's phone number. I dialed and got his room.

"Yo, what's up? How are the farmers' daughters?" Paul joked. I could see the smile on his face.

Without letting him get a word in edgewise, I told him in detail about my new found energy. "You can meet Mick Jagger or any star for that matter with my new position as the "World's Greatest DJ." I wanted to convey the energy I felt. After all, he was my twin brother, who better to understand all of this?

"As a matter of fact, Donald Trump will be working for *me* soon," I cockily stated.

"What are you smoking up there?" he asked me, taken aback by what he heard. "It's ten o'clock in the morning. If you're doing coke, that's bullshit," he yelled into the phone.

"Coke? What the hell are you talking about? I'm not doing coke, there's no need for any of that crap. You're an asshole. I'm trying to let you in on some pretty amazing things and you ask me if I'm on drugs?" I hung up in disgust. Of all people, I was sure he'd be excited for me. I was so upset I forgot to pack the puppet with the rest of my gear.

I hurried downtown to the Greyhound bus station, paid for my ticket, sat on the bench and waited for the bus marked "Hazelton" to arrive. My destination was Fort Indiantown Gap. "The

Gap,"is where most of the Pennsylvania National Guard and Army Reserves conduct weekend training. My cousin Keith and my future brother-in-law Harry were the lead officers. A typical weekend drill was to drive armored vehicles into the wilderness, and practice reconnaissance maneuvers. Friday night we packed gear and gassed the vehicles for the rest of the weekend. By breakfast time on Saturday, we would be out in the woods doing drills.

After what seemed like forever, the Greyhound finally arrived. As I slung my bag underneath the metal compartment. The bus was completely empty. I sat by myself in the back and listened to music. The ride gave me time to work on the mathematical equations necessary to drill to the earth's core. The book said the average radius from the core to any point on the earth is 3,959 miles. I calculated I could a have the hole for the transmitter box drilled by spring, no problem. I couldn't wait to show Steve these brilliant plans.

I thought of how my radio show would sound and how best to get my message out to the masses so they could realize the power of the no-sleep theory. Up to this point the only real radio show I'd listened to was Howard Stern. He was kind of my inspiration for using a radio show format to reach the masses in the first place. His show it's funny because he's surrounded by people from all walks of life: It suddenly hit me--his talent is putting people on his show who represent the people he makes fun of. That way he relates to everyone, without offending anyone in his audience. They're in on the joke. Brilliant! I began to think of who would be the lucky person to be my co-host for the show. It would be much easier to convey my message if I had someone with whom to talk back and forth. But if I wanted to follow Howard's model, it would have to be someone who represented the people.

I had it! Chrissy Ferraro! She'd be perfect. She's the funniest and most beautiful girl I know, and her name even sounds like a rock star! Chrissy with a C was our homecoming queen in high school. Just as Howard has an ability to reach everyone, she has a gift for floating in between social cliques as gracefully as a ballerina dancing across a stage. She could be making party plans with the stuck-up girls from the cheerleading squad one minute, then hacky sacking with the burnouts the next. Chrissy is a tomboy who grew quickly into a beautiful woman, but didn't think of herself that way. If you mentioned anything about her being homecoming queen, she'd probably burp or pretend to stick her finger in her nose to counter the image. A few minutes at the lunch table with her and you'd probably be thinking of her the rest of the day. My buddy Todd was dating Chrissy and all of us were jealous.

She'd be perfect for my show. If anyone could help me reach the masses, she could! The bus made a stop and I ran out to the pay phone, I had to tell her the good news. I pulled my book with phone numbers out of my bag. I figured I would at least leave a message. I'd be careful not to mention the transmitter, because it was too soon. I still needed Steve's help and I'd already said too much. The phone rang and rang.

"Hello," a soft voice answered as if I'd awakened her.

"Chrissy, it's me Pete Barnes, how are you? Can you talk?"

"Pete Barnes, how the hell are you, kiddo? Are you up in Bloomsburg with Krissy Evans?" I could tell she was smiling by the tone of her voice.

"Actually, I really don't know where I am, I'm headed to a drill weekend for the army and I got off the bus to call you. But that isn't important. I have major news for you. Tell me, who's your favorite band of all time?"

"Uh—I dunno, the Doors?" she said as a question.

"No, I mean a band that's alive."

"OK, I guess off the top of my head I'd say the Talking Heads right now."

"Good pick! If you get on board now, you will have the power to call up David Byrne and say come over and he's gonna run!"

"What, why?" she said, totally baffled.

"I can't give all the details, but we're on the brink of changing the world. The speed of business, world hunger, we can solve it all with a simple solution I uncovered. Sometimes I can't breathe thinking about how mind blowing it all is and how simple. The answer was here all along! We don't have to sleep anymore! I'm afraid someone might be listening or I'd tell you more about how this will all come together. Let's just say the U.S. military will be on our side. With your beauty and humor and my brilliance, we can't fail. I said without taking a breath. I had to get back on the bus soon.

"I'm sorry, Pete, but I have no idea what you're talking about," she replied with confusion.

"Don't worry, Chrissy, this is going to be the most amazing thing you've ever been a part of. What I'm talking about is a type of radio show that will broadcast around the world, everyone on the planet will listen to us! Can I count you as my co-host for the show when it gets off the ground?"

"I'm headed to the University of Dayton in two days to start school. Aren't you supposed to be in school too?"

"Yeah, I'm in Bloom, but none of that will matter. You're going to be so big you can't even understand it yet. When things get rolling, I'll send a plane and you can commute whenever you want. Think Howard Stern times a million."

"How are you going to get plane, and who's Howard Stern?" she said, still not understanding what I was talking about.

"I'll get you details later, are you in?" I asked, trying to lock in my co-host before the 400-pound bus driver climbed back into the driver's seat.

"Pete, you're not making much sense to me, but if you can get a plane, I'd be up for checking it out. Sounds fun." She laughed.

That's all I needed. "Kick ass, partner! I'll call soon with more. Gotta run!"

I slammed the phone and raced to the bus as it started to move slowly out of the parking lot. I banged on the side of the bus and quickly made it to the front; the massive bus driver opened the door with a look of scorn on his face.

With the co-host slot locked in, ideas for the show came one after the other. My hand was getting sore from writing. A sudden lurch brought me back to my surroundings. The bus had finally pulled into the fort and I walked about a half a mile to our building.

As I walked in, people gave me hugs and high-fives. I could hear comments from the back of the room, "Hey, look, 'Duffel Bag' decided to join us, how nice." "Nice hair private." "Duffel Bag" was the nickname my brother and the other guys in our army unit called me because I never ironed my uniforms correctly.

The barracks were plain: two stories of wood plank floors lined with long rows of metal bunk beds draped with green blankets. A light bulb with a string dangled above each bed. It's the kind of place where flip-flops are mandatory and bringing along an extra roll of toilet paper never hurts. I threw my gear in the corner and in less than two minutes my buddy Greg handed me a cold beer. It went down smoothly.

Because the bus had arrived late all the work for the day had already been finished. I could tell by the red cheeks and blood shot eyes the party had started without me. Friday night's refreshments consisted of a trashcan filled with iced Rolling Rock, cheap booze, stale hard pretzels, and bags of potato chips laid out on a fold-up table. Who could ask for more?

From upstairs someone yelled, "Locker races!" These races were a weekend drill ritual. The new guys always went first. Bill Hartman and I were the most recent to return from basic training so we strapped on our helmets. Two narrow staircases separated by a thin wooden wall lead to the second floor. Metal storage lockers were emptied and placed at the top of the stairs. Each person lay in a locker on his back, feet first. The doors at the bottom of the staircase were held open, and a small patch of grass outside the doors was the intended landing zone. The person who traveled the farthest was declared the victor. Most of the time, however, the locker would veer off course and hit smack into the side of the door.

Once I got into the locker, the door shut, and pitch black followed. The next thing I knew, I felt a push, then a deafening sound of wood slamming against metal. For a moment my stomach dropped and there was silence, a second later, crash! The locker stopped moving, but I didn't. My knees cracked on the locker door and I could feel the helmet strap yanking my neck. Then a roar came from the crowd. We both made perfect runs. What a rush!

After several people took turns zooming down the stairs in the lockers we returned to the main room to have a few beers. In the corner a few guys seemed fascinated by what I said. To warm up the crowd I tried my best Eddie Murphy impression on them.

"I got some iiiiiice- cream, I got some iiiiice-cream...an' you can't have any...cause you on wellllllllllllfarrrrrrre," I went from impressions, to explaining my reasons why people never had to sleep again, without taking a pause. My audience was in hysterics. I had no idea the laughter was pointed at me not with me.

"Where the fuck did he come from?" asked a guy who'd been transferred to our unit over the summer.

"Damn, the white boy is higher then a motherfucker!" another guy said spitting out his beer and laughing.

After I'd "killed 'em" in the barracks, I went outside to have a smoke. I took a seat on the steps next to Sergeant Dan Walker, somebody who everyone in the unit admired. His nickname was Sergeant Otter because he looked and acted a little like the guy from Animal House. He's the type of guy who could party all night and still outperform everyone the next day.

"So where'd you go to basic?" he asked as the smoke came out of his nose and mouth.

"Paul and I went to Fort Knox," I proudly replied.

"No kidding, I did too. Fort Knox blows," he laughed.

After sharing stories about basic training, Otter left to get a fresh beer and use the bathroom.

54

Alone, I stared at the beauty of the stars; the first time I'd sat still in days. The slow burning ash of my cigarette was the only visible sign I wasn't frozen in time. In that moment something happened.

A high school teacher once told our class humans only use a tiny fraction of their brains. As I sat numb to the outside world, a wild tornado blew open the doors of my mind and gave me access to one-hundred-percent of my brain matter. In less then a second, the universe's infinite glory made complete sense. I understood solutions to the world's most complex problems, and answers to ancient riddles suddenly came to me. My whole being screamed in pleasure as if my body had aligned in perfect harmony with the vibrations of the cosmos, yet I never uttered a sound. My laugh echoed over and over in the chambers of my head with each new realization. The intensity of what took place was inconceivable, yet I was extremely calm.

A godlike presence funneled information through me. No light beamed from the sky, no face, no words spoken, only a feeling of intense exhilaration. I was like a child standing in the center of a gigantic blizzard with my arms stretched wide and tongue out catching snowflakes. Each crystal revealed a mystery and then vanished instantly. I couldn't keep pace with the storm, but I savored every millisecond. Abruptly, I was yanked back to earth, when the embers of my cigarette connected with the flesh of my index finger.

"Damn it!" I screeched like a little girl.

"Damn it what?" Sergeant Otter asked as he opened the screen door. He sat down to have another cigarette. I tried to describe what had happened. "Slow down man, you ain't making any sense," he said.

As I began to put into words the storm of energy that had just engulfed me, I remembered a part that might translate to him. Peter Church, a fellow soldier had died tragically in a house fire almost exactly a year before. During the trance or whatever I'd been through, my spirit wrapped in an embrace of sorts with Pete Church's, long enough that he could pass on a simple message. He simply communicated that death was nothing to fear as long as your soul was genuine.

Sergeant Otter and Peter Church were best friends; he was there the night Peter died. I don't know if he believed me or was just happy to hear Peter's name, but he smiled.

"You know you're okay," he slurred his words as he put his arm around my shoulder. "You're gonna make it around here, 'cause you're as fucking weird as the rest of us."

I pushed open the door like Paul Revere warning everybody about the Red Coats. I wanted to share Peter's message with everyone. I selected a small band gathered around the trash can filled with beer and began to ramble incessantly. A kindergartner, telling of his day's activities, would have put together a more cohesive story. I babbled on about the secrets of the universe, while they gazed upon me, puzzled by my incoherence.

I must have started to annoy the crap out of my listeners. Out of nowhere, they swarmed me, picked me up, and put me into a locker. I thought I was headed for another locker race. After a few minutes in the locker, I got pissed. Enraged, I began kicking and yelling at the top of my lungs. My arms were wedged so I couldn't reach the handle. I kicked as hard as I could. Finally I did some damage with a kick that bent the metal; enough to get some attention. They didn't know what to make of my frantic behavior. My attitude had swung from elation to sheer rage without skipping a beat. As soon as they yanked me out, I calmed down.

It sucked I couldn't get the common people to understand me—as brilliant as I was. Emotions were uncontrollably spilling out. My chest heaved, as I tried to keep from crying again. Finally I pulled myself together and held back my emotions with all my might. Taking long breaths, no tears came out, but my voice gave me away, as I tried explaining the situation to my cousin Keith and future brother-in-law Harry.

They'd been drinking and assumed I was drunk too. Once I said my piece, they brought me back inside, sat me down on a bunk and told me to get some sleep. I continued to explain how the transmitter would work, but they walked away.

Sergeant Otter came back and took the bunk next to me.

"Are you awake private?" he whispered.

"Yeah," I said back.

He showed me a quarter full bottle of tequila.

"Good, cause hell if I'm gonna waste this," he said, taking a swig then handing it to me.

We sat across from each other passing the bottle back and forth. It was nice to have someone who understood me. Just before morning, a new idea struck me which seemed a perfect way to deliver my message.

No matter how late you worked or stayed up partying, in the Army National Guard, you had to make first formation. Miss first formation for any reason and expect to catch serious shit. This ritual came at roughly 4:30 a.m. Soldiers were required to shave and be in proper uniform, after a head count daily duties assigned. This was my opportunity to finally get everyone to understand me at one time.

As the standard cassette recording of a bugle played, people grumpily stumbled out of bed in the darkness. As planned, I crouched behind a window overlooking first formation. With shaving cream still on parts of his face, Sergeant Otter came up to make sure I held my position.

"Wait until I call out the first name." he said softly so as not to draw attention.

"Don't worry I got it." I replied.

The moment the sergeant began to call the names for roll call, I cracked open the window and with all my might bellowed in my best Robin Williams impression, "GOOOOOD MORNNNNNNING FORT INDIANTOWN GAPPPPPPP!"

Everyone looked up, baffled, except for Sergeant Otter, who bent over laughing out loud. No one else laughed. Cold, cold silence filled the air. A colonel from another unit had come to inspect our morning formation. Before I got out a word of my monologue, the colonel and Keith, who'd been leaning against the downstairs door, rushed up and grabbed me.

"What in the hell do you think you're doing, son? Do you know where you are?" the colonel asked, looking at me, as if I was a Russian spy.

I was dazed; why didn't anyone laugh? I didn't get it, what went wrong? This made no sense. As Keith and Harry ushered me away I smiled taking take bows.

Beyond a doubt, everyone present knew something was drastically wrong with Pete Barnes. I wasn't a drunk at a party. There were no excuses. What I thought were breakthrough ideas others saw as irrational sentences running together. When I got on a roll, I sounded like movie soundtrack that was chopped up into pieces then edited back in no particular order and sped up.

I thought to myself, "What's wrong with these people, don't they at least get the humor?" I struggled with a madness I didn't understand. The manic behavior picked up on my normally outgoing personality traits and blew them into cosmic proportions. My actions and speech patterns were my body's alarm system blaring to the outside world.

Keith and Harry brought me into the officers' meeting room. Sitting on a metal chair with my arms folded, I believed I was superior to them in every way. That morning was the first time anyone treated me as if I was sick.

As they questioned my behavior, I compared myself to Superman. No one understands Superman; he just comes down to the average person's level when he needs to talk to humans. He cares and helps whenever he can. I felt the same way. I'd have to come down to their level so they wouldn't get in my way. When I let them in on my secret, to build a transmitter to the core of the earth they did not even react. I concluded, some people simply weren't able to handle my superior intelligence. I did my best to say, "Yes sir, no sir."

As plans "to teach the world to sing in perfect harmony" formed in my head, alternate plans were made to get me to a shrink. Keith had been on the phone with my sister and mom to try and figure out what to do with me. Finally, after what seemed like a long debate on the phone in the room adjacent to where Harry kept a close watch on me, they decided to drive me home.

CHAPTER FIVE

Day Seventeen: A Long Walk Off a Short Pier

September 17, 1989

Sitting directly across from Josi in her living room, I noticed a change. Grey hairs were now replacing my mom's original color of light brown, making her look older than her fifty-five years. Harry and Diane stood across the room and Josi sat in a large chair. They looked at me like I was a circus freak. My eyes were wild and I was raving a million miles a minute about all my adventures. I was obsessing about getting back to Bloomsburg.

"If you don't get me back there I will tell the world you're standing in the way of the revolution. I mean Valley fucking Forge is our backyard, don't you guys get it?" If George Washington had skeptics like you trying to stop him from greatness where would we be today? I reasoned, in my plea for a ride back to school.

I could not understand why driving me to Bloomsburg was such a big deal. Nothing anybody said mattered, unless it fell in line with my plans to go back to Bloomsburg, to become the "World's Greatest DJ." My ability to listen had vanished. I was like a record player on high speed and the needle was stuck.

"Can you just shut up for a minute?" my sister screamed at me with tears streaming down her face.

"Don't yell, you'll make it worse," Josi barked at her.

Harry, my sister Diane, and Josi talked among themselves. They kept saying something was wrong with me. This conversation was driving me crazy; I was being treated as if I'd been kicking puppies or something.

"I don't know what to do. We have to get him to a doctor," Josi cried. "Do you think someone slipped him some drugs?" she asked Harry.

"Who would slip a guy drugs?"

Fed up, I stormed down to the basement and paced like a caged animal. I sat on the couch with my head in my hands, furious they didn't understand, I could change the world.

I could hear them arguing above me. Each one offered a different explanation of why I was acting so strangely.

"Let's just get him to Paoli hospital and see what they say," Diane said.

My mom was in shock, seeing how fast I'd morphed from a normal teenager to a person out of control.

"It's Sunday night for Christ's sake, what are we going to do? I knew these boys should never have joined the army at their age!" she said to Harry.

"Don't look at me. The army has nothing to do with this," Harry was offended by her comment.

They seemed so concerned and I didn't have a clue why. Did they think I was going to run upstairs with an axe? I mean, I was in the best physical shape I'd ever been. "You guys are the sick ones!" I yelled up with a laugh.

In reality, I looked gaunt, my eyes were bloodshot from lack of sleep, and I smelled funky. Unlike a person with a broken arm who has screaming pain, I had no internal warning that I needed help.

Harry walked down the stairs cautiously, not knowing what to expect. He seemed the most reasonable of the three. He talked, while I began to do as many push-ups as I could, to prove I was in perfect health.

"Can't you see I am fine, I'm better than fine!" I looked up.

"Your sister and mother believe there might be something wrong."

"What crap!"

Harry sat on the couch and watched me push the floor. "Hey, I don't think anything's wrong with you, I know you're a smart guy. They're just worried, you know women. If you see a doctor, he'll tell them you're all right, and then I'll drive you back to Bloomsburg tomorrow morning, deal?" Harry offered.

"I'll drive you back to Bloomsburg tomorrow morning," were the only words that registered.

After a short drive to the hospital, I sat in the waiting room for what seemed like forever. A man walked in and introduced himself as Dr. Stanley Miller. We walked down the hall to an empty emergency room. The doctor pulled back the curtain and offered me a seat. Harry, Diane, and Josi stayed for the introduction, then Dr. Miller politely asked them to leave. Mom blurted out a bunch of questions, but Harry gently escorted her out. I was put off because the doctor wore civilian clothes. No white smock, not even a damn stethoscope. No animation entered his voice, he seemed genuine. To me, this conversation was a tennis match. With my superior brain waves, I knew I couldn't lose. I was ready for any questions he could slam over the net. The problem was, the doctor wasn't playing. Instead, he turned on the ball machine so I could play myself.

"So Pete, how are you feeling today?" he asked with a smile.

"I feel great, better than ever. Can you believe they're wasting your time like this? I have so many things to do. Can you help me get back to Bloomsburg? Seriously, they won't take me back, but I have a lot of work to do there. Do you know anything about radio transmissions? Well, not exactly radio transmissions. You see I have this project to finish, it will change the world and how we communicate. Do you realize I can broadcast my radio show into your head?" I said, without taking a breath. Surely he saw my genius and would help me get back to school where they needed me most.

He nodded his head so I knew he understood.

"Pete, can you tell me the last time you slept?" Dr. Miller asked.

I continued to explain how the human race didn't need to sleep at all. I figured he must have dealt with other people, graced with super intelligence before. After hearing me out for a long while, he left to talk to the peanut gallery, who'd been waiting in the lobby. I was sure Harry would be gassing up the car for Bloomsburg. I was happy my family would finally understand I was healthy.

The ride home wasn't what I had expected. I told them how Dr. Miller thought I was an amazing guy, and he knew why I had all of this extra energy. No one replied. When I asked about going back to Bloomsburg the next day, they agreed--to shut me up for a few minutes.

A five-year-old on the night before Christmas couldn't have been as excited as I felt. Bloomsburg had become a fantasyland in my head, filled with endless possibilities. I lay on the couch in the basement, thinking over and over about drilling to the center of the earth. Not only would I be the "World's Greatest DJ," but my team would be the first to get to the earth's center. I could see the headlines on newspapers around the world. This would be the biggest story of the century. The Wright Brothers had nothing on me. I continued to keep detailed notes in my notebook about the dimensions of the box and the pressures it would have to withstand. I figured out the language translator aspect of this device. It would be so easy. I'd have a bi-lingual person from every language listen to the show telepathically, and then broadcast their own version on a channel for each language and dialect. Once the box was planted in the core, I'd teach people how to tune in their minds. Luckily, I was able to stay up all night dedicating the hours necessary to get the idea into motion.

By 5:30 the next morning, I'd showered and packed. I waited eagerly for everyone to get up. Harry slept on the couch, dead to the world. I kept making noises around him, in hopes he would stir. He just mumbled for me to go back to bed. Josi came downstairs at 7:30 a.m. and made coffee. She hadn't slept. "Go to bed until Harry wakes up or you're not going anywhere." Her tone was of a parent talking to a two-year-old, forceful, instilling a touch of fear. I retreated to the basement and waited impatiently. Each second seemed like an eternity. I looked forward to bouncing all my ideas off Harry on the ride back. Most of all, I just wanted to hear the words, "Pete, let's go."

Finally I heard Harry talking to Josi. I ran up the stairs. Harry, Josi and Diane sat around the kitchen table looking at me as if

I had a dress on. I asked Harry with eagerness, when we could get on the road.

Josi said, "You're not going back to Bloomsburg. Dr. Miller wants to do some more tests today."

"Bullshit! You guys are liars!" I raged.

How dare they go back on their word? "Who the hell are you to tell me what to do? I'm eighteen!" They didn't waiver. I stormed back to the basement.

It took me about two seconds to figure out a plan. I had to go to the third-floor loft in order to get to a phone where no one could overhear me. I cautiously made my way up the steps and called my friend Krissy's dorm room at Bloomsburg.

"Krissy?" I whispered.

"Yeah, who's this?" she replied, taken back.

"It's Pete. I don't have a lot of time. There's a good chance the phones are tapped. I've uncovered a secret so big, I'm pretty sure the people who control the radio towers and satellites might try and stop me. The good news, when I get back to Bloomsburg and complete my project, I'm going to have the biggest party the world has ever seen; it's going to be epic. Van Halen will be there, MTV, and you can invite the entire campus." I talked fast hoping they wouldn't trace the call.

"Pete Barnes?" she said, "Is this a joke?"

"Listen Krissy, this is no joke. I need a huge favor, the world depends on it, I depend on it," I said, as if I was James Bond. "Do you have your car up there?"

"Yeah, why?"

"Please meet me at the McDonald's at the Pocono exit on Northeast Extension, I'll explain more later, but this is an emergency,"

The highway exit was about 120 miles from my house and forty miles from Bloomsburg. She seemed confused, but Krissy agreed to get there by 5 p.m. and wait for me. Bingo! I was ready to get the hell out of this house. I could have kissed her right through the phone. I still wasn't sure how I was going to make it, I just said, "Don't worry, I'll get there."

I walked calmly down the stairs. Harry had been searching for me. We crossed paths in the living room. I said goodbye with a smirk and then made my way out the back of the house through the sliding glass door. My sister was upstairs, and my Mom yelled at Harry to keep me in the house. I leapt over the railing and started to run. It took a second for Harry to react, but then he came after me, dashing out the door. Harry sprinted as fast as he could. Over my shoulder I could see him closing in on me; my leg plunged in a small ditch. I fell flat on my face. I scrambled to get up, desperately trying to run again. I could hear heavy breathing, then arms wrapped around my legs. We both stood up, Harry held my shirt. He tried to reason with me and loosened his grip for a split-second. I broke away and I took off as fast I could. This time Harry couldn't keep up. I knew he'd forgive me eventually.

Common sense said I should have been dead tired, but I'd never run so fast in my life. I'd heard stories about people having super-human strength; I felt the same type of mysterious adrenaline surging through my veins as I raced through the suburban neighborhood. A lady watering her yard looked at me like I was an escaped convict. I ran over fences, through a playground, into the woods headed for the closest entrance to the Pennsylvania Turnpike.

Out of breath, Harry ran back into the house, "Diane grab the keys to the car, he ran off."

"What do you mean he ran off? He's not a dog," Diane said, confused.

"Don't blame me. I tried to stop him and he just kept running. Listen, I saw where he went. Your mom can stay here, in case he comes back."

Just then, Josi walked up from the basement in tears.

"What's this!" she yelled out loud. "What the hell's wrong with my boy? This doesn't make any sense!" she said, handing my sister my notebook.

Diane sat on the couch and flipped through my tattered notebook. She had no idea what to make of it. The notebook was filled with indiscernible text, riddled with diagrams and strange cartoon faces. In large capital letters, words like UNIVERSE, BRILLIANT, NO-TIME, and TELEPATHY were scattered throughout. On the last page, WHY DON'T THESE STUPID MOTHER- FUCKERS UNDERSTAND!!!!!! took up almost an entire page.

"Mom, what exactly did the doctor say last night?" she asked as she handed the book to Harry.

"He said, it's a chemical imbalance in the brain. I don't even know what the hell that is, but Dr. Miller said it's common. Pete might have to be hospitalized for weeks, to get well. He's eighteen, so he has to admit himself. He wanted us to bring him back today--so he could convince him the hospital was the best place for him and I could get his things ready," Josi said all of this in between wiping tears from her eyes.

"Listen, Mom, stay here in case he comes back. Harry and I are gonna go look for him, don't worry, everything will be fine," Diane said, hugging my mom. She grabbed her car keys and they hurried out the door.

Within about fifteen minutes I'd made it to the tollbooth area on the highway. There was a truck stop adjacent to the entrance. I'd never hitchhiked before, but my only option was to land a ride. I had no money and my bags were back at the house. All of this was inconsequential to me.

I felt great! Nothing could stop me. I just needed a ride. The lady in the booth contemplated whether she should call the cops. On the side of the road, a man added oil to his beat-up 1981 dark-green Citation. I went to see if I could give him a hand and snag a ride. He wore a long beard, dirty jeans and an old black-and-white Aerosmith t-shirt. I asked if he needed a hand. I was wearing new jeans and a navy blue collared shirt. He looked at me as if to say, "Who the fuck are you, the friendly neighborhood turnpike fix-it man?" Turning away from the car, he flicked the ash off his cigarette, scratched his well-rounded beer gut.

"Hey, do you mind if I get a ride? I'm headed back to Bloomsburg."

He started laughing. "Bloomsburg? My cousin went to Bloomsburg, I used to party up there all the time."

Then he paused and thought for a second, "Hell, I'm only going to Allentown, but I'll drop you off there, if you want."

"That would be awesome," I said shaking his hand.

"Name's Clyde. I smoke in my car, if you don't like it, too bad." I couldn't stop thanking him as we got in the piece-of-junk car and took off.

Back at the house, Josi sat at the kitchen table trying to think of a good way to convince me to go to the hospital. The phone rang.

"Mrs. Barnes, I know you don't know me too well, but this is Krissy Evans, Pete and Paul's friend from high school. I go to Bloomsburg with Pete."

"Krissy, of course I know you. You're the sweet redhead who went to the prom with our Brian," my mom said, trying not to breakdown. She knew all of our friends' dates and girlfriends by name.

"I don't know how to explain this, but something is going on with Pete."

"Krissy thanks so much for calling, we're looking for him now. It's some kind of chemical imbalance and we have no idea what happened."

"Well, he called me a little while ago and asked me to meet him by five on the highway near the Poconos. He sounded off the wall; I didn't recognize him at first," Krissy said with concern.

"Christ," Josi pulled the phone away from her mouth. "Sorry Krissy, we thought he was in the neighborhood somewhere,"

"I'm going to drive there, Mrs. Barnes. If he comes home can you call me in the next half-hour? It'll only take me about forty minutes to get there."

"Krissy, I'm scared," Josi replied.

"He told me to meet him at the McDonald's," Krissy added.

"Please wait till he gets there. I'll meet you, if I don't find him first."

"Of course, everything will be fine. Pete's a smart guy Mrs. Barnes," Krissy said in attempt to calm Josi down, but the phone call had freaked her out.

"Thank you, Krissy, I'll see you there. I'm leaving now." Josi left a note for my sister, got in her car and took off.

Clyde and I were blazing down the Northeast Extension of the Pennsylvania Turnpike. The floor of his car had a layer of crusted dirt adorned with crumpled cigarette packs, a couple of cassette tapes, and a sausage egg McMuffin wrapper.

The constant rattling in the back made me feel like the car could rip apart at any second. He turned the radio to *94 WYSP*, the Philly station that carried the *Howard Stern Show*. Howard and Robin Quivers read the news of the day to finish the show.

"Howard's the best show in the country, but not for much longer. Did I tell you I'm going to be the greatest DJ on earth? By the time I'm done, people won't remember Howard Stern.

Like me, he had selective hearing. All he heard was the word DJ. This was a great excuse for him to re-live his short-lived career as a DJ in Allentown.

"I got promoted from board operator to overnight DJ when the morning guy overdosed and was out for six months in rehab," he said blowing smoke out of the crack in his window.

"Have you heard of *Rock 107, For Those About to Rock?* We were classic rock before the 'classic.' AC/DC, the Stones, CCR, Alice Cooper, you know, good music." He said in his deepest voice.

Out of nowhere, he turned the radio volume down and started singing.

"'I'm on a highway to hell! I'm on a highway to hell!' Now there's some great music, not like this gay Cure shit they play today."

"Yeah, I hear ya," I said to make him feel good. I liked the Cure.

Clyde changed the subject. "Hey, you don't have any buds on you, do you?" he asked with his fingers rifling through the ashtray overflowing with cigarette butts. As he did this we swerved off the road and nearly hit the cement barrier.

"No, sorry, but you should have been at some of the parties at Bloom they had whatever you wanted," I said.

"I can imagine, I miss those days." Clyde smiled and looked out the window.

I loved smoking pot, I'd done it since I was fourteen. That's when my friends started drinking and doing a lot of things we shouldn't have. But I never really considered us pot heads or druggies. Almost all of us played sports, had jobs and got decent grades. Right now, I felt like drugs and drinking were beneath me. My mind was too powerful for them. My purpose was greater.

"You know the funniest thing we did at my old station?

I said nothing because I wasn't sure that it was a question.

April Fool's Day, it had to be fifteen years ago. We had the whole stupid town convinced the Stones were playing a surprise show in the park downtown. This was back when it might have been believable that they would just show up somewhere. I mean cars lined up, people were everywhere. These idiots believed Mick Jagger would play for free in Allentown. Man, I'll tell you, there are some morons in this town," Clyde laughed.

Time flew by. We were both having a blast: he reliving the good old days, while I boiled over with thoughts of what was to come. He dropped me off at the Allentown exit. I thanked him hurriedly, and made my way back onto the turnpike. I put my thumb in the air and walked down the entrance ramp.

As long as my plan to build the transmitter and broadcast to the world was not being challenged and I was moving closer to Bloomsburg, I was happy.

Cars and trucks whizzed by for a half hour before anyone pulled over. Eventually, a Mazda Protégé with a Penn State University sticker on the back windshield, stopped. The passenger-window rolled down and I could see a girl and guy who looked about my age.

"Where are you headed?" the driver asked.

"Bloomsburg. Do you know it?"

"Yeah, it's on our way."

"Cool. I saw the Penn State sticker on the back." I said, as they opened the door.

I jumped into the backseat and we were on our way. They introduced themselves as Melanie and Dylan. The girl had gorgeous natural blonde hair. Dylan looked as if he had walked out of a J. Crew catalogue. Unlike Clyde, they didn't have any good stories, so I felt obliged to provide the conversation. I figured I'd let them in on what I knew.

"Did you know we'll have no need for radio stations or television soon? You'll be able to tap directly into the mental channel of your favorite entertainer. I'm headed to Bloomsburg to build the transmitter to make this possible. I won't even need a microphone; I'll broadcast directly into people's minds."

I didn't want to give too many details, in case they would try to steal my idea. But I wanted to give them the big picture.

Leaning over the seat, I asked, "Melanie do you want me to read your mind?"

"Um, like what do you mean?" she said without turning around.

"We can use telepathy to read each other's minds. I've been practicing for a while," I said with pride. "I'm pretty sure it only works when both people are trying."

"Um, that's okay, I don't want my mind read right now." she said sarcastically.

"How about you, Dylan?" I asked.

"Na, I had mine read yesterday, I don't want to overdo it, ya know."

I laughed, "It's safe anytime."

"Seriously dude, just chill," he said, also without turning around.

About ten minutes after I'd given them my precious secrets, Dylan turned to Melanie and said, "Oh shit, I forgot my book bag." He looked back at me, "I'm sorry, we have to turn around and go back."

I looked around the back of the car and there were two book bags next to me. I pointed this out. "No, I left my other book bag at my house." He quickly pulled the car to the side of the road and stopped. "Hey, be careful. If we see you on the way back, we'll pick you up." Dylan said as he pulled away. Melanie never said goodbye or even looked in my direction. Oh well, I thought to myself.

I soon found out this was a difficult stretch of the highway to get a ride. There were no exits nearby, cars whizzed by at over seventy miles an hour. I was still about forty-five miles from the exit where Krissy was meeting me. After a couple minutes of sticking my thumb in the air, I kicked some garbage out of my way and began to jog.

The scenery was breathtaking – the colorful fall leaves carpeted the rolling hills. I sucked in the air, the smell of fall rushed into my nostrils. My strides got longer and faster. After about a quarter mile, I'd stop then start the process all over. I'd recently finished a 17-mile road march in basic training with sixty pounds of gear on my back, so why couldn't I run the rest of the way? I wasn't taking into account I was on the highway and I didn't have any water, food, or running shoes. But there I was cruising down the highway like Forrest Gump. I don't know exactly how far I went, but it had to be at least ten miles before I began to slow.

I developed a monster thirst and I was sweating buckets. I looked around for anyplace to find a drink. A church in the distance was the first building I'd seen in miles. Cows and billboards had been my only companions until then. I jumped the guard rail and sprinted through a field of tall grass. A cross, thirty feet tall, hung on the side of the building. Pulling the door open, I got a freaked-out feeling like I was going to walk in and see chickens being sacrificed. It was eerily quiet as my feet stepped on the shinny linoleum tile squares. I tipped toed in and looked for a water fountain. In doing so, I ended up surprising two teenage kids who sat at a table in what looked like a kitchen. One of the guys who was tall and skinny with a soft voice, stood up.

"Can we help you?" he asked.

"Do you have a water fountain?"

They pointed me to the fountain and watched me from the doorway as I practically sucked it dry. After quenching my thirst, I ducked my head under the chilled stream and soaked the back of my neck. Refreshed and ready to go, I said thanks.

"Where did you come from," the other guy asked.

I was tempted to mess with them and introduce myself as the second coming of Jesus, but I was on a mission, so I refrained. I needed to make time so I gave them the fastest version of my mission without reveling and details about the transmitter. Like everyone else they seemed perplexed. I just figured people would not be able to truly understand until I got the transmitter working and everyone connected to the show.

"Hey guys, thanks for the help, I've gotta keep moving to catch my ride." I made my way to the door.

"Peace be with you," the tall one said.

"Same to you!" I yelled as the large door slammed behind me.

I hopped the fence and was on my way. My dry throat was the only thing that had slowed me before. I felt no need to hitchhike anymore; I figured I could run the rest of the way with ease. I trucked down the road like a wild horse. I had God on my side, I thought jokingly, how could I go wrong? But my perception of God had changed back on the steps of the army barracks. The notion of one god in the heavens seemed a bit like Santa Claus to me. We were all gods and our particles all connected. So in fact I was a God in the sense that we are all connected and are one being in the universe. I was a vessel that would help connect the collective consciousness, so all humans would know that the need for sleep was a lie. I felt so privileged to be the one who would rid the world of sleep! I wondered, if like in Sunday school when we reenacted the crucifixion of Jesus, would people reenact my journey back to Bloomsburg in the same way?

All sorts of thoughts and sounds played in my head like a cool mix of music on an imaginary Walkman. I sang aloud whatever song popped in my head. The Doors' *Roadhouse Blues* was my current selection.

"'I woke up this morning and I got myself a beer!'" I sang as loud as I could.

There were a few glorious clouds in the sky that kept my mind occupied as I made out stories from the formations. I ran along the highway as fast as I could, until my legs stopped me. I felt like a soldier riding a magical horse through the mist carrying vital information to save the troops from eminent danger. I'd run until my legs gave out, I'd walk for a minute or two then gradually start sprinting again. The pavement felt soft and rubbery. I never came to a full stop. A primitive Tarzan voice in my head said, "Go there!" The need to get back to Bloomsburg was so nagging I'd have put my body through any torture to get there.

I passed a big green road sign, it read, Pocono exit ten miles. The sign put new life into me; I was so close! I'd be at McDonald's in no time.

I could hear the noises that the *six million dollar man* makes as he runs through the woods as my strides quickened. When I saw tiny billboards in the distance get larger I imagined I could easily leap over them. I would scoff at the radio towers in the distance, pointing at them, like Babe Ruth pointing at center field in Wrigley Stadium. "Your days are numbered you big ugly scars on the land!" I'd scream and laugh out loud.

I imagined my future radio fans lining the streets, cheering and clapping for me to finish the race. But with no one in sight, I ultimately relied on pure willpower to drive me on. My energy far outpaced my body. I was frustrated with the simplicity of my body as a vessel. There had to be a way for humans to move faster. I could feel the inefficiencies of my muscles and skeleton working together. I was pretty sure, I'd find a way to reengineer the entire human transportation system.

I was again in need of some water. I spotted a cluster of monopoly-style houses just off the highway. As I fumbled my way over a huge fence, my pants got caught on the barbs at the top. I pulled my leg over, tearing the bottom of my pant leg, and fell over to the other side. My landing was a little rough, but I got up, dusted myself off. The first group of houses I saw were about a hundred yards away. I made my way over as fast as I could without running. A middle-aged woman stood by a hedge wearing yellow rubber gloves and holding garden shears. Stumbling over the uneven ground, I made my way to her. She spotted me well before I got close enough to say anything. I waved as if I was the postman about to drop off the mail.

"Ma'am, would you mind if I had a drink of water from your hose?" I paused realizing my voice was hoarse. "I'm not too far from where I'm headed, but I don't have any water left," I said politely when I did get close enough for her to hear me.

"Well, sure, go right ahead," she said with equal graciousness.

"My name's Pete Barnes, nice to meet you." "Sheryl, Sheryl Hassinger. Where are you coming from?" she asked me as I drank from the hose. A man stepped out of the house onto the back porch.

"Valley Forge, I'm headed to Bloomsburg University," I replied.

"Valley Forge? How did you end up here?" She spoke like a schoolteacher.

"I had a ride most of the way, but they left their books back..." She stopped me. "Son, you just wait here while I get you a glass of ice water." As she walked toward the house she turned and said, "Are you hungry? Of course, your hungry."

She walked inside, and the man on the porch stepped forward and introduced himself, "Hi, I'm Jeff, you walked off the highway?"

"Yeah, just a little thirsty. It's hot for September,"

"Hot? I was just about to ask you where your jacket was."

He was right, a nice breeze had picked up. I'd been running for so long, my body was overheating.

"So, tell me the truth, are you a part of some kind of fraternity prank or something?" he said as he sat down, in a cushiony lawn chair.

"What do you mean?" my voice improved.

"Come on, I went to college too," he smiled. "I pledged Phi Kappa Tau at the University of Boulder back in '52. I remember they made us share a bottle of Jack Daniels and dropped us off in a field, blindfolded, ten miles from campus. We had until breakfast to make it back to the house," he paused, looking up trying to recall a detail.

"Oh yeah, we had to bring back a live chicken. Come to think about it--that was one of the funniest nights of my life."

"Oh, no, I'm not in a fraternity, I'm starting a project that will revolutionize the worlds communication system, I have to get back to get my plans together."

"I know, I know, we weren't allowed to say anything either." He winked.

I offered up the tale of how my day started and what I had to do to get here, minus the part of running away from my house. After a few minutes, Mrs. Hassinger interrupted with a peanut butter and jelly sandwich and a tall glass of water. The crunchy peanut butter was my favorite; I ate it in two bites. The Hassingers were kind people.

"Now, Pete, you listen. I am not letting you leave unless we know someone's definitely picking you up at the McDonald's," Mrs. Hassinger insisted.

"Call whoever you need," Jeff handed me a portable phone. I had the number for Krissy's dorm in my pocket. I got the main desk, they transferred the call and her roommate Robin answered. She seemed nervous and talked fast.

"Krissy left a long time ago, what's going on? Where exactly are you right now?"

"I'll be there soon. In case she calls back, will you tell her I'm almost there?"

She asked again, "Where are you exactly?"

"About ten miles from the exit," I told her, remembering the road sign.

"Clorinda and Krissy are definitely going to be at the McDonald's. They left forty minutes ago," Robin said.

"Perfect, thanks. Things are amazing, I can't wait to get back to Bloomsburg. We are going to have the biggest party the campus has ever seen to celebrate what I've discovered. Your invited, spread the word!" I answered excitedly.

"Party? OK, sounds great." She said confused. "Be careful," were her last words before hanging up.

As I handed him the phone, Mr. Hassinger said, "You better get going before it gets dark." I had thought he would want to invest in the transmitter when I told him about it, but I guess his brain was too small to comprehend the brilliance of what I'd revealed to him. His tone had the polite but cold manner you get from someone behind an airline counter. I guess I was beginning to overstay my welcome. I said goodbye and headed back to the highway. Glancing back, they waved and I returned the gesture.

Knowing Krissy was on her way, I moved like the Energizer Bunny. Ten minutes later the glorious day faded as the sun disappeared behind the hills. I wondered if people would look back on my journey back to Bloomsburg as a historic moment. Maybe kids would get a day off from school.

So far I'd covered over a hundred miles in total. Headlights began to pop up as if to tease me. I moved faster as dusk finally turned to darkness. I stayed focused on reaching my mark. I was hell-bent on seeing Krissy sitting there, sipping a frosty milkshake. Everything else would work out, once I got there. The trucks seemed louder and grew bothersome. I chugged down the road with my head down, trying to avoid the lights which became more frequent. Then I rounded a corner and looked up. There was a brilliantly lit sign about a hundred yards away. It screamed at me, "POCONOS NEXT EXIT." I jumped up and down as if I had just won a race, and yelled at the top of my lungs, "Hell yeah, I made it!" Nothing except a huge eighteen-wheeler could have stopped me. I felt no pain on my last leg of this all-important pilgrimage.

In the near distance was the McDonald's sign. The golden arches never looked so good. I checked to make sure no cars were coming, and then bolted across the highway. I leapt over the waist-high guardrail and began to slide down the embankment, almost falling on my face, I caught myself at the last second. My legs spun until I made it halfway across the parking lot. Little did I know, Josi was on the opposite side of the building trying to convince a state trooper to look for me.

"Officer, please help me. He's somewhere on the highway, he'll get killed," she pleaded.

"Ma'am, our troopers have been alerted and I'm afraid that's all we can do. If your son is stopped on the highway, he can be detained for trespassing on federal property. I know you're upset, but we can't do anything until we spot him," he said, not knowing anything else to say.

A trucker overheard them. "Miss, if you'd like, I can call in on my CB and have them keep an eye out."

"Oh, would you? Thank you!"

I walked into the restaurant feeling utter satisfaction. I'd run more miles then a marathon runner in dockside shoes and I felt winded but amazing. Krissy and Clorinda jumped up when they saw me. Krissy gave me a bear hug.

"Your mother is worried sick about you."

"I know, isn't it messed up? Everyone's acting so strange." I sounded confused.

At this point, Clorinda ran outside and grabbed my mom by the arm. Trying not to make a scene, she whispered loudly, "He's here, he's inside."

Krissy hugged me again. My mom ran in with the cop walking calmly behind her. Everyone in the McDonald's had their eyes on me.

"What's she doing here?" I asked Krissy accusingly.

Josi was going to ruin everything. My mood went from relief to anger the second I saw her walk through the door. I backed up, looked for the door. I'd come too far for this shit. My mom cried, and they all pleaded for me to wait.

I didn't know what to think. Bloomsburg was forty miles away; it would be impossible to hitch a ride at night. Krissy asked me to sit down with her while we figured it all out. Cautiously, I sat in a booth. Krissy had asked Clorinda to come with her because after the phone call she was a little afraid of me. Clorinda, barely topping five feet, was a funny choice for protection.

My mom looked horrible, her hair was messed up, and the lack of sleep showed. She came over to the booth, insisting I get in the car, and she'd take me to Bloomsburg. I looked at her with disgust, "Yeah, just like Harry was going to do this morning," I expected a laugh from Krissy but she looked at the ground. Krissy then asked if she could talk to me alone.

"Pete, I have no idea what's going on, but you need to calm down. The cop said he could arrest you right now for walking on the highway. If you promise to chill, Clorinda and I can drive you back to Bloomsburg. Everything will be fine." Krissy said as sternly as any eighteen-year-old could, while staring into the face of a friend she could hardly recognize. She was the only person I trusted at the moment. I knew my only choice to get back to the promised land was to go with her.

"You swear you'll take me back?"

"I promise," she said as a big smile took over her face.

"As long as I can go back with you and Clorinda, I'll go," I said in a serious tone, as if I had other options.

Once the decision was made for Krissy to drive me to Bloomsburg, everyone settled down.

Josi ordered food for me, but I couldn't eat. I didn't know what to expect next. Josi and Krissy talked privately and I sat with Clorinda staring at me. I could tell she was nervous as she made small talk.

The three of us piled into Krissy's car and pulled out of the parking lot. Josi's car practically touched Krissy's bumper. The state trooper stayed behind my mom's car, but he pulled off the next exit. The back seat felt good. Krissy and Clorinda sat up front. Words flowed like silk from a spider the whole ride back as I spoke about all that was to come. The girls both rolled their windows down, I didn't even pause to realize how bad I smelled after running so many miles. I was just surprised how quiet the girls were.

Then we passed the sign: *Bloomsburg 1 Mile*. We pulled up to the campus and I couldn't sit still. I felt like everything would finally work out. I began to thank Krissy and Clorinda profusely. Krissy drove slowly around the narrow roads up to my dorm. We came to a stop just outside the main doorway to the building. My mom's car pulled behind us, and we all got out. "Thanks for keeping your word,

I will never forget that," I said to Krissy and Clorinda, then bolted inside. Krissy walked to Josi.

"Mrs. Barnes I don't mean to upset you any more then you are but something is really wrong with Pete. Nothing he's saying is making any sense. He barely took a breath the whole ride." Krissy whispered.

"Oh Krissy I know, I have no idea what to do. I wish we could've gotten him in the hospital back home."

"I have to go but you have my phone number, if there is anything I can do to help let me know." Krissy said giving my mom a hug.

"Yeah me too." Clorinda said as they headed back to their dorm.

"You two are angels," Josi said holding back tears.

The resident manager, Dan Crenshaw, and a security guard came from around the corner and stopped me as I walked into the lobby. The security guard asked Dan, "Is this the guy?" My mom had called Dan earlier from the McDonald's and told him what I was saying about getting back to Bloomsburg. He recognized my mom from the day I'd moved in.

"It's great to be back," I shook their hands like a politician running for office.

Dan asked me to sit down. He claimed he was doing me a favor by letting me stay overnight in the dorm, and I had to meet with campus officials in the morning.

I had no idea what he was talking about. I only wanted Josi to leave. Then I could get back to my room and everything would go back to normal. Soon I wouldn't need to live in this dorm because I'd be rich beyond my imagination. When I bought my apartment off campus I wouldn't have to deal with these jokers anymore. I nodded my head and agreed with everything Dan said.

As he spoke, I daydreamed about how to decorate my new apartment. I'd have a bar in the corner with a six-foot tall lava lamp and a huge bedroom with a waterbed. The bar would be stocked with every alcohol imaginable. I'd host "telepathic world parties"-- people around the world could connect to my mind and see and hear everything going on. Guess who's not going to be invited to the party? I thought looking at Dan and the security guard. I tried to contain myself from busting out in laughter because they all seemed so serious.

"Do you have a phone I can use?" Josi interrupted.

"Yes, over at the front desk," Dan pointed. He continued to lecture me as she went to call my sister.

"   ack at Bloomsburg, he's with me." Mom said as
)icked up.

)rining him home?" Diane asked.

"He won't come, this is all so crazy. I'm getting a hotel room. I don't know what I'm going to say to the office tomorrow. I can't believe this is happening." My mom held back tears. "I'm supposed to meet with people from the university and they're going to help me figure out what to do."

"What to do?" Diane said sharply. "He needs to be in a hospital. I talked to my friend Cathy today whose sister Annie had a chemical imbalance. She said Annie talked the same way Pete did, she said it's a mental illness."

"I know he has to get looked at, I just don't know how to get him there without him taking off again. He is eighteen, he has to go voluntarily. Oh Diane, I don't know what to think. I'm going to wait until the morning when the university people can help me. I'm so scared, but he seems to have calmed down now that he's back here." My mother sighed.

"Harry and I will be ready to help in the morning."

"The truck driver who was helping me at McDonalds said I should get a drink, I think he was right." Josi laughed.

"Maybe you should. But call us in the morning and be careful," my sister said before saying goodbye.

I was getting fed up listening to this dork from the dorm tell me what I could and couldn't do. My eyes darted from Dan to the security guard at the door, then back to Josi on the phone. The last thing I heard him say was, "So, we'll see you at 8:30 in the morning?"

I faked a smile, "Sure, in the morning." I wanted to get to my room. Disappointed with my mom, I walked right past her and gave her a look of disgust. If she'd let Harry drive me here this whole scene could have been avoided.

Eventually the security guard, Dan, and my mom all huddled by the front door. "Mrs. Barnes, we'll keep a close eye tonight. All the doors have alarms after ten. Also, we've told the students on the wing to look for any strange behavior. This isn't the first time this has happened. He's going to be fine once he gets to a hospital."

"So everyone in the dorm knows what's going on?" Josi asked.

"We can't legally discuss illnesses, but we warned them Pete may not be himself. I think they made their own interpretations," Dan replied.

"Well, I booked a hotel nearby. What time should I be here tomorrow?"

"I'll have everyone here by 8:30. I think the best thing we can do is to talk him into going to Geisinger. It's a great facility about ten miles from here."

"But I can't stay here, I have to work. It would be much better if I could get him back home."

"I understand Mrs. Barnes, but based on his obsession with Bloomsburg it might be the only hospital he agrees to. If it helps, they have a great reputation for treating mental illness."

"I just want my boy back. This scares me so much. Did you hear him? Did you see his eyes? That's not my boy. He was normal when we dropped him off here." Her voice rose from a whisper to almost a shout.

"I know this must be hard, Mrs. Barnes. We'll be here in the morning. Mrs. Masterson, the school psychologist, is driving back from a conference at Penn State tonight. She'll be able to make suggestions; she knows a lot about this kind of thing," Dan did his best to make her feel better.

"Go and get some sleep, it's the only thing you can do."

"Sleep? How can I sleep when my child's going nuts?" Josi said defeated.

"I'm sorry, but there's nothing we can do right now. I've seen students go through this before. If he gets to a hospital he'll get better," Dan assured her.

"I'm sorry, I'm just freaked out," Josi apologized.

"Don't worry ma'am, I won't let anything happen to him," the security guard said as he opened the door.

I headed back to my room.

"Hey man, what the hells going on?" Steve caught up with me before I made it to my door.

"What do you mean?"

"The dorm manager and RA told everyone on the floor to tell them if we saw you," he said with excitement. "Is everything cool? Matt said you were in some kind of trouble before he left for his lacrosse tournament," Steve said as he followed me to my room.

"Well if trouble means becoming the 'World's Greatest DJ,' then yeah, but these assholes have no clue. They're just angry I'm moving out of here soon to my own apartment anyway," I grumbled as I opened my door.

"Oh, don't worry man. I'm with you—it's cool," Steve said, backing off a little.

"Steve, I have to show you my plans for the transmitter. It's gonna be easy."

"Great, but you might think about grabbing a shower. You stink." He laughed.

I took his advice and hopped in the shower. The water pounding on my back felt wonderful. But when the hot water reached my ankles, I felt a burning sensation. Two large open blisters on my heels looked gruesome. When the pain subsided and my body adjusted to the water temperature, I scrubbed off all the dirt from the long day.

I dried off, got dressed and sat on the edge of my bed. I needed something to do. I realized I still had a bunch of girls' phone numbers I'd collected. I randomly called all the numbers to see if anyone would come over. While I dialed I looked in the mirror and noticed how good I looked. Sherry, the attractive girl I met in line registering for classes was first to pick up the phone. I had a tremendous urge to get laid and I was prepared to say anything to get her to come over.

"I'm sorry, I have to study tonight. Can we do it another night?"

"Too bad. After tomorrow, I have to spend a hundred percent of my time on my new job as a DJ."

"DJ, what do you mean DJ?" she said, intrigued.

"Just come over for an hour, I'll tell you about it."

"Just for an hour, I have to study at some point."

"An hour, I promise,"

"Okay, okay, what dorm are you in?"

I explained how to get into the dorm via Steve's window—which was standard procedure by now.

I ran out of the room and down the hall to Steve's room where I quickly explained the situation.

"Does she have any friends?" Steve asked.

"It's too late to ask, next time, I promise. Can you help?" I pleaded.

"Why not? But next time she has to bring a friend."

While I waited for Sherry, Steve's roommate Tom came in the room and I could not help but unveil my plans. Relaying the ideas into layman's terms was difficult. Their back and forth looks to each other confirmed my ideas were captivating but slightly over their heads

"Hey this guy is great!" Tom said as he made a cuckoo sign by twirling his finger to the side of his head when I looked out the window for Sherry.

. We heard a tap on the window. Tom opened the window so Sherry was able to crawl in.

"Hi," she said in a shy I-just-crawled-through-a-stranger's-window way.

She wore black jeans and a purple and gold Bloomsburg sweatshirt. Sherry looked better than I'd remembered. Steve and Tom gave me a look of approval. I grabbed Sherry by the hand, looked around to make sure the RA didn't see her, and then ducked into my room. We sat on the bed making flirtatious small-talk. Within five minutes, the ice was broken and we began kissing. I was groping her, like she was the last woman on the planet. She stopped me, "Hey, slow down." We continued kissing and I tried to take her sweatshirt off. She blocked me with her hands as she kissed me. "I've never had such an incredible urge to touch a body." I whispered in her ear and it was true. I hoped the heat of the moment would change her mind. Instead, she seemed upset.

She backed away saying, "Listen, this was a bad idea, we barely know each other." I went to her and kissed her hard against the wall. She kissed me back but then abruptly pushed me away. "Pete, stop! We just met." I backed off and apologized, "No more touching, I promise, let's just talk." Not wanting to be alone trumped my feelings of horniness. Positioned in front of the door, I pleaded with her to stay a little longer.

"I can stay for a little while if you promise you'll behave."

"Promise!" I said as she sat back down, but this time on my roommate's desk chair.

Sherry had expected a quick make-out session as a nice diversion from her books. Instead she got me, who began to scare the crap out of her.

"Is something wrong with you?" she asked with concern after I spoke for a few minutes.

"Why does everyone keep asking that?" I said puzzled.

Sherry got the play-by-play of what had happened to me in the last few weeks. I could not stop talking. It seemed like my mind was moving faster then my mouth but I was compelled to get it out. After a while, she stopped me.

"What's the time?" Sherry asked.

I looked at my watch. "It's a little before midnight."

"I have to get back to my dorm, I have class in the morning." She opened the door.

"If you need to go," I said disappointed. I woke Steve and his roommate to sneak her out the window.

I realized I'd left my plans at home; I started over with a fresh notebook. I stayed up the rest of the night redoing the diagrams and made sure all of my calculations were correct. This version was better than the original.

At 7:30 a.m., I still worked furiously writing in my new notebook. RING, RING…. The phone startled me. Josi said to meet her in the lobby in a half-hour and dress nicely. I went through every combination of shirts and pants I had. I wanted to look my best. The half-hour had passed and I continued to try on clothes. A loud knock on the door surprised me, and I glanced at my watch. "Ah, shit." I knew I was in trouble. I opened the door to find Dan, with his arms crossed. "Everyone's waiting for you downstairs." After one last look in the mirror, I decided the tan pants and maroon Rugby shirt from my high school team would have to do. I always felt I was pretty damn cool wearing my team shirt. "Bring it on," I thought, as Dan escorted me to the lobby.

Josi stood in the lobby. "Good morning," I said in a cheery tone. She looked worried. Dan pointed and we both followed him down a hallway to a short staircase leading to the basement. I'd never been in this part of the dorm before. The yellow walls were stained; they hadn't been painted in years.

I stepped through the door with trepidation. Several older people stared as I walked in. Dan pointed out a seat. Then he introduced everyone in the room. Bloomsburg's resident psychologist, Mrs. Masterson, coldly said hello and shook my hand. A large man stood in the corner of the room, he wore a gray sports jacket too small for his large frame. A gray-haired lady named Jean Carpenter, the vice president of Student Affairs, said hello from her seat.

The metal chairs made an irritating noise as people adjusted to get comfortable. We sat around a large, hard, plastic folding table. A gray divider was half-pulled out in an attempt to create two rooms from one. The security guard from the night before walked in wearing civilian clothes, sipping a cup of coffee. I didn't have a clue where this was going. One thing I knew for sure, when a group of adults got you in a room to ask questions, it never turned out well. Despite my anxious feelings, I had no doubt my superior intelligence would help me to prevail.

The psychologist who seemed to be in charge of the witch-hunt talked to the others and acted as if I was invisible. My mother sat next to me. She leaned over and whispered, "They want to help, they're only going to ask questions to find out what's best for you. Please try to listen."

Mrs. Masterson spoke like a police officer who'd pulled over a speeder. "So, Peter, why do you think you're here?"

I thought they wanted to know about my plans, to broadcast to the world. So I proceeded to unveil portions of my plan to provide a glimpse of my far superior intellect. I struggled between letting them in on my plan and not wanting to divulge details, knowing full well I couldn't trust this group. I figured they probably wanted to put me in a doctoral program because of my genius.

After about twenty minutes, I'd helped them to a speedy decision. My mother pleaded with me to stop. She was crying, "Don't you know what you're doing?" Mrs. Masterson said impersonally, "Peter, it's our decision that it would be best if you see a doctor at Geisinger Hospital." Dan followed her as if they had practiced this. "They have specialists who can help you."

She was arrogant, I hated Mrs. Masterson. I put my hands on the table and fumed. "I'm fine! I told you more than enough information. Einstein couldn't explain all of his theories to people like you. You're too ignorant to understand what I know!" I shouted.

"You can't talk to me that way!" Mrs. Masterson replied.

"I want out of here now!" I said as I stormed to the door. The security guard went for the door. Mrs. Masterson was in my line of direction as I raced to beat the security guard. I tried to dodge her but we bumped shoulders as I tried to quickly maneuver around towards the door. She screamed as if I had punched her or worse.

"Pete, please calm down," Dan Crenshaw attempted to diffuse the situation. He touched my shoulder as I stared down the security guard. "Who the fuck are you to tell me what I can and can't do? I am a million times smarter then any of you idiots." I yelled at Dan.

My mom pleaded, "Stop they're trying to help. You're sick, can't you see?"

"Listen, they're going to evaluate you at the hospital. If everything you say is valid, then you are welcome back," Dan said with calmness and conviction.

Every person in the room was on edge.

"You're right, we don't understand everything you do, but we want the experts to help us figure it out," Dan continued.

"You can go to Paoli Hospital or Geisinger, just a few miles down the road," Josi implored.

Dan struck a chord in me. I wanted to push the fat ass security guard out of my way and make a break for it, but I knew that meant immediate expulsion from Bloomsburg, my promised land. I tried to calm down. "They're just going to ask questions?" I asked.

"Yes," Dan replied.

"Will they know what I'm talking about?" I asked.

"I sure hope so," he said as a relief filled smile broke across his face.

I thought, if what they said was true, the doctors would understand me, and I'd be out in no time. After all, the doctor in Philadelphia was the only one so far to recognize my brilliance. This could be my only chance to put my critics to rest.

"If I go today, and they say I'm fine, I can come back to Bloomsburg?" I said, backing away from the door.

"Of course, this is just temporary until the doctors ask you some questions," crowed Mrs. Masterson who stood arm and arm with the security guard.

Believing I'd be out later in the day I agreed to go. "Take me to Geisinger, or whatever it's called."

Josi was so relieved, she turned to me and gave me a hug. "Thank God," she sighed. "I need to go get some things; I'll meet you at the hospital." Then Josi shook Dan's hand, but never spoke a word to Mrs. Masterson. Everyone left the room, except for the man standing near the divider and the security guard from the night before. The guy with the sports-jacket was a town cop out of uniform. I sensed he shared my uncomfortable feeling about this situation.

The two men escorted me out the backdoor of the dorm to a waiting car. The town police offered a ride to ensure I didn't run away again.

I started to climb in the backseat. "No son, you can get in the front. You're not a criminal," the cop said as he opened the front door.

I moved to the front and a few minutes passed, which seemed like an eternity as other students passed by gawking.

Slater and Kirk stood on the corner talking with a group of girls. They noticed me and I was horrified. I couldn't explain to them what was going on.

The two came to the window. Slater joked, "Yo, Pete, what's up? Did you kill someone?" Kirk followed. "Don't worry, we have your back."

The security guard moved them out of the way.

"Can we get going?" I asked the cop.

"In a minute, I'm waiting for the rest of these clowns."

Mrs. Masterson talked with Dan Crenshaw. I smiled at her, knowing I'd be back soon. She smiled back, knowing I wouldn't.

The car pulled away from campus and we headed onto a highway. "We're on our way. We should be at Geisinger within ten," the officer said into the hand mike. There was a strong smell of Old Spice aftershave. My back was sweating, my rugby shirt stuck to the plastic seat covering. My anxiety grew in direct proportion to our proximity to the hospital.

We pulled up to a side entrance of the hospital and I walked in flanked by a nurse and a hospital orderly. They pointed me to an empty waiting room. Framed pictures of mountain scenery were highlighted by the florescent lights. Curtains were draped halfway over two windows overlooking the parking lot. There was a phone in the room. I thought maybe Krissy could talk to the doctor and vouch for me. Josi walked in the room with a nurse in tow. They handed me papers to sign. I rifled through them, but I was too anxious to read.

"These papers give the doctor permission to see you," the nurse said. "I need you to sign these pages and initial these," she said flipping quickly through the pages." I signed them and made my way to the phone.

I got Krissy on the line.

"Krissy, you gotta help me. Something's wrong," I whispered.

"What's wrong?" Krissy asked.

"Well, I was taken to a hospital in a police car," I said nervously.

"Your mom said a doctor was going to talk to you?" she said.

"Why did they take me to a hospital when I'm perfectly healthy?"

"Is your mom there?"

"Yeah, she's here. I signed some papers to see the doctor, but I have a bad feeling. All these people are around, what do they want from me?" A nurse now stood in front of me.

"What kind of papers did you sign?" Krissy asked.

"I don't know, just some stupid insurance forms."

"I'll get in the car. Where's Geisinger anyway?" she asked.

Just then a nurse got too close for comfort.

"You're going to have to say goodbye. It's time to see the doctor."

"I'm on the phone, do you mind?" I mocked her serious tone.

"Yes I mind. This is a hospital and you have to obey our rules. Please say goodbye and come with me."

I didn't know what to do. I didn't want to piss off the nurse and have her tell the doctor I was an asshole, but I didn't want to be treated like a kindergartener.

I covered the receiver for privacy. "Krissy, they're telling me I have to hang up. Please come, and can you call John Kelly my friend from basic training who came to the party with us. I'm at Geisinger. Get here soon, please," Then I hung up.

"I'm not going anywhere until I see Krissy and John," I said to my mom.

"Why can't you make this easy?" Josi replied. Next to her sat a bag packed with clothes.

"What's the bag for?" I asked. She didn't answer.

Two male orderlies came into the room. "The doctor wants to see you now," one said.

"I'm waiting for someone," I clutched the arms of the chair as they approached.

"Come on guy, don't make this hard on yourself," one of the orderlies tugged my arm.

I pulled away. "Get the fuck off me asshole! I'll go when my friends get here!" My heart pounded. This was worse than when the fraternity guys had my puppet.

I jumped out of the chair, pushed the closest orderly out of my way and ran as fast as I could. A mix of hospital orderlies, nurses and cops stood at the end of the hallway. I'd gone the wrong way. I was right where they wanted me. They walked towards me shoulder to shoulder like riot control. Obviously they'd done this before. But I wasn't going to make this easy for these bastards. What a disaster--I was trapped. I punched, kicked, bit, even spit. I wasn't thinking, just reacting.

They used a modified leather weight-training belt to wrap my arms. The strap tightened across my chest rendering my upper body useless. I could barley move my hands. The belt made my chances for escape slim. I still had my legs and they continued to flail.

The guards and nurses called to each other. "I got him." "Watch his legs." Every so often I would break free and run down the hall. Each time, they surrounded me and had to start over. I felt like a bull in a rodeo.

"Don't you dare hurt my boy. I never agreed to anything like this!" Josi shrieked from the other end of the hallway.

A nurse tried to comfort her, "Mrs. Barnes, they won't hurt him. They're professionals. It's the only way."

The elevator door closed, I was gone.

There was no room to kick in the crowded elevator. I was stuck. The cops and nurses took turns giving me advice. One of the cops said, "Just settle down, you're making it worse." I think his shins were still stinging from one of my attempts to break loose. Another guy who was an orderly said, "Everything's going to be fine if you calm down. The doctors are cool."

I panted, out of breath. I didn't know whom to trust or if that even mattered. The commotion made me feel like I'd jumped into a blender and someone pressed puree.

"Are you all so stupid you don't understand how brilliant my ideas are?" I pleaded.

The battle had momentarily taken the wind out of me. By the time the elevator doors opened, I stopped fighting. I was shuffled off the elevator and escorted into the hospital wing. Everyone and everything seemed to be moving in slow motion. Over my shoulder, I saw a large room with a few people standing around. A lady laughed and pointed at me. This set me off on another cycle of rage.

"Why are you looking at me?" I shouted at the top of my lungs. I pulled away from the guards and orderlies and made a break for the doors. The door was locked and I was surrounded within seconds.

"Get the hell off me. I won't go anywhere, I promise," They guided me around the corner into a hallway.

Except for the fat lady laughing no one in the room looked in my direction anymore. I was hurried down the hall into an examination room. They propped me up on a long table with the familiar annoying strip of sanitary paper crumpled underneath me. My arms were still strapped. I wished this was some horrible dream and I'd wake up any second.

"Listen, I'm not going anywhere till I see a lawyer. This is bullshit! Who the fuck are you people anyway? Get me out of these straps." I demanded. "My friends Krissy Evans and John Kelly can explain everything, can you go get them?" No one in the room responded. "Does anyone hear me?" I growled.

Veins on my head felt like they would explode. Then a nurse asked, "Are you going to calm down so we can take off the restraints?"

"Can't you tell I am calm?" I said laughing hysterically.

"Listen, you're only here for testing and observation so the doctors can diagnose what's wrong with you," she continued.

"Don't you idiots get it? It's you who must have the problem. I'm FUCKING FINE! When do I get to see the doctor?" I asked one of the orderlies.

After the female nurses left the room, two male orderlies came in. The first orderly promised to take off the leather strap if I took the pills he handed me. I wanted the straps off, so I opted to take the pills. After I swallowed them, he was true to his word. He told me he would put the straps back on if I got out of control. The tone of everyone's voice changed now that we were in this room. They treated me like an injured animal. The two orderlies asked me to follow them into another room. I obliged.

I stood in the center of the new room, the orderlies hurriedly walked out. The door shut with a resounding clank of a bolt slamming into place. Trapped with no idea why, I went ballistic.

I ran to the door, there was no handle. I had to jump up to see out a small window in the door. Three chairs sat empty in the hall, I could see nothing else. I turned to examine the room. The dull white walls made of a heavy coarse cloth blended together. Large buttons like ones found on a couch or a heavy pillow fastened the padding to the wall. The only object in the room was a mattress on the floor covered with the same thick material. The room itself measured about twelve-by-twelve feet. There was no toilet. I felt my pants, I had no belt. I couldn't believe it. I'm in a loony bin!

The time I spent in this room was the apex of my mania's intensity. My ability to hold onto lucid thoughts vanished. My thought process resembled a film chopped into little pieces and re-edited in no particular order.

"A goddamn outrage!" I yelled. All my plans, all my visions are going untested, unfulfilled! These types of rooms were for insane people. I accepted the fact the average Joe couldn't grasp the big picture until my radio broadcast reached the masses. I needed out immediately in order to build the transmitter and get on the airwaves. This confinement both enraged and baffled me.

My stockpile of energy was sharply focused on getting out. I attempted to peel one of the large white buttons out of their sockets to see what was behind them. Not able to remove the button I turned my attention to the door. I examined the small glass window as a possibility for escape. The handle on the outside of the door was out of reach and the glass was about four inches thick, this put a kibosh on any hope of escaping out the door. I banged on the window screaming for anyone to open the door. From the outside I looked like a dog locked in a car at a shopping mall, barking ferociously at people passing by.

"Has the rest of the world gone mad? I've just graduated from basic training for Christ's sake," I thought.

I was so confused. One minute I'm in college drinking beers and meeting beautiful women, the next I'm treated like a basketcase. "So this is what it's like to be wrongly persecuted." I shouted. Jesus was feared and misunderstood by people in power, and look what happened to him. I wasn't hanging on a cross, but who knew what these people had in store?

"How'd everything get so out of hand? Did I deserve this?" I wondered.

I gazed towards the ceiling. I'd been concentrating so intensely on possible escape routes, I never saw the camera. "A freaking camera; what a fool I've been, all this wasted time."

Now I understood!

"It's all been a test!" The radio people must have set the whole thing up. What a perfect gag! "A padded cell for a private audition, whoever came up with this is brilliant!" I laughed so hard it hurt. They must be watching somewhere. Maybe they're getting me ready for *The Tonight Show*. I wondered if the cops were in on it too. I'd figured out their secret and now I'd give em a hell of a show.

To persuade the masses to never sleep again I would need entertainment value in my show to keep them coming back for more! I figured everyone loves impressions so I did the ones I thought I could do the best. My favorite was Pee Wee Herman's *Hamburger*

Dude from Cheech & Chong's *Nice Dreams*. I had a few more up my sleeve. I went from a knockout Ronald Reagan impression to doing an Oriental voice arguing with a customer about delivering the wrong order of eggrolls and wonton soup. I threw in my Eddie Murphy in *RAW* for a little spice. My finale, Randle Patrick McMurphy and Cheswick demanding cigarettes from *One Flew Over the Cuckoo's Nest*. I kept screaming for Nurse Ratchet. "Where the hell are my cigarettes you bitch?" When I ran out of material, I settled down for a short time and then I'd repeat my act over and over. I cracked myself up.

I was killing, but no one came to the door. This audition was turning into a torture chamber. Why wasn't anyone coming? Whoever was behind this was in for a long fight. After delivering more then ten hours of the best show ever, I began to break down.

I looked to the camera and pleaded for a phone so I could call Howard Stern. If anyone would understand my plight, it would be Howard. When my shouts received no response I decided I needed to go straight to the top.

"Get me a direct line to the president! I know my rights," I demanded.

I looked through the window again. The thick glass made it blurry but this time I could see people sitting in the chairs. The true reason I was locked in this padded room hit me. The TV show Jeopardy! Why hadn't I thought of this before? Those people outside the window were the *real* Jeopardy contestants. The contestants on TV were fake stand-ins, the entire show was a facade. The actual show was a broadcast vehicle created by a small group of super-geniuses, so they could secretly extract knowledge from the smartest people on earth. This room was designed to siphon brilliant thoughts from my mind. Each time the phony contestants on TV pushed their hand buzzers, the people in the hall zapped my brain. I had good reason to believe Alex Trebeck was behind this whole fucking thing. I didn't even get to be on TV. This devastated me.

Pacing back and forth, pushing on the walls, I continued to develop a list of reasons for my lock-up. One theory was based on a premise that my humor was a virus threatening to wipe out human race. When people heard my show they laughed uncontrollably. If they told another person what I said it would cause a catastrophic domino effect. Was my being in here saving the world? Would they keep me here for the rest of my life? I sincerely hoped I hadn't killed anyone.

When all the possible reasons as to why I was stuck in this room were exhausted, there was nothing left for me to do but yell until I had no voice left.

"I WANT OUT! I PROMISE I WON'T HARM ANYONE!"

I jumped up and down on the mattress and grabbed for the camera, which was inches from my reach. Next, I turned my attention back to the door. The dull thud of my body told me thick steel was behind the white padding. I pulled the mattress next to the door and tried flying drop kicks. Finally someone came!

115

An orderly the size of a MAC truck opened the door a crack.

"Hey kid, I've worked here three years and I promise you the door isn't moving."

A nurse, who followed directly behind the orderly, handed me a tray. A tired sandwich, juice, two slices of an apple, and three pills were on the tray. The orderly stood guard against the door.

"I'm not eating any of this bullshit until I get out of this room," my voice barely audible.

The nurse explained, "It's your choice, but eating the food and taking the pills are the types of things you need to do to get out of this room. Do you understand?"

My eyes shot between the orderly at the door and the nurse. As I pondered making a move for the door, the orderly caught my glance.

"Don't even think about it. Even if you were to pull off a miracle and get by me, two other guys are waiting outside, and they're bigger than me." The orderly pointed his thumb over his shoulder.

"The doctor will explain everything after you eat and take these pills," the nurse repeated calmly.

This was the first time anyone had entered the room. My desire to get out was greater than any fear of the little pills. So down went the medication. They sat there while I ate and didn't say a word.

After a few bites of the stale sandwich I nearly spit it out on the floor.

Having succumbed to the demands of my enemies, I thought this meant freedom, in an hour or so. Wrong again. No one came back. I began to get outraged again.

"You are fucking lying assholes! I am not kidding; you're done! Ha! You fools don't even know you're cut off from the world's new communication system!"

I still couldn't figure out whether the roving eye in the ceiling was a friend or foe. But it now drove me nuts. I gestured for the camera to watch me. I grabbed my crotch Michael Jackson style then did my best attempt at a moon walk. A strong urge to relieve myself gave me a brilliant idea. This surely would bring about my exodus. Moving a foot from the edge of the door to get a good angle, I began urinating at the crack of daylight under the door. My intention was for the pee to stream under the door crack, make its way down the hall, and find its way to one of the nurse's shoes.

Most of the puddle stayed on my side of the door. Either way, I made a mess. Once again I found a way to get their attention.

The same orderly from before came within a minute. I was laughing hysterically. He shook his head, "I've seen worse. You're the one who has to sleep here. We were about to take you to the real bathroom, but I guess you don't need one now." One sweep of the mop and he was gone again. When he mentioned sleep I realized my watch had been confiscated when I came in. The lack of outside windows made it impossible to tell day from night.

"I'm sorry, I'm sorry! Come on, let me out! Please let me out. I've got a lot of things I have to do. Why do you have me in here? I didn't get my chance to call a lawyer!"

I leaned against the padded wall and hyperventilated like a child trying to explain how he'd got the crap beat out of him. This was the last in a series of rants which had lasted for two days. I knew this was no DJ audition. No friends or family were coming. I felt like crying, but there were no tears left.

Frustrated, beaten down, out of breath and utterly exhausted, I slid down and plopped onto the floor. For the first time in weeks, I had no energy. I curled up, put my head on the edge of the mattress and closed my eyes. My final thought was, at least I gave them a run for their money.

Then something remarkable happened. I fell asleep! This was the first real sleep I'd experienced since the first days of college. Of the kaleidoscope of thoughts in my head, it never occurred to me that the only way out of this room was to fall asleep. It had to just happen.

CHAPTER SIX

Day Twenty Two: "Wing 7"

September 22, 1989

After what seemed like an eternity, I opened my eyes to a gentle hand on my shoulder. I jumped back. Where am I? What's going on? Who are you? This all ran through my head, but nothing came out of my mouth. I squinted, as my surroundings came into focus. My body ached. I felt like the typical soap opera character waking up from a coma after a dreadful car accident. The only thing missing was the beautiful nurse yelling, "Doctor come quick, he's waking up!" Instead of the beautiful nurse, two odd-looking guys were peering at me, as if I had just arrived from outer space.

One wore a pale green doctor's outfit with a black and gold nametag that read: Dr. Verrett, Frank, Psychiatrist. Judging by his pronounced crows feet, I guessed he was in his forties; but the Doctor's most prominent feature was his bushy eyebrows which looked like they'd been taped to the rim of his glasses.

119

The other guy looked like he walked right off the football field. He stood six foot three and had what the military calls a high and tight hair cut. His nametag read David Owens. He carried a wad of keys that would make any custodial engineer water at the mouth with latchkey envy.

I pictured the night before, when I pissed on the floor. For a second I cowered like a child who'd been caught misbehaving. This sense of sheer embarrassment had been absent for weeks.

Dr. Verrett smiled and asked in a cheerful tone, "How are you feeling?"

"I feel like crap." I croaked, my voice was barely audible.

I realized the two men weren't there to punish me. A wave of relief rushed over me, as if I'd woken from a nightmare.

The orderly handed me a tall glass of water and I gulped it down. He asked "Do you want to get out of this room?"

My eyes lit up. "Yeah, sure!"

Stepping out of the padded room I gazed to the left and then to the right, checking out my new environment. I felt in no immediate danger, just an uneasy restless sensation. The confusion outweighed any feelings of being threatened. I was moving forward, unable to hold firmly onto the recent past.

I'd compare my situation to the end of a roller coaster ride. The thrill of twists and turns still lingering as the cars jerk to a rest and shoulder straps rise. Now enjoying the security of solid ground, I failed to realize I wouldn't leave this amusement park anytime soon.

Dr. Verrett, David the orderly, and I walked down the hallway past the nurses' station. A solid sheet of Plexiglas buffered the nurses' station from the main room. The place looked like a human terrarium. The concrete walls were painted off-white and had outdated medical posters hanging on them. Next to the counter was a yellow smiley face painted on the wall. Below it in quotes read, *A frown is a smile turned upside down.* All the orderlies and nurses dressed in white pants and pale blue shirts. Photo IDs were clipped directly under their nametags. A nurse behind the counter did not look up from her paperwork when we walked by.

About twenty feet down the hallway, we made it to an open room. A group of odd-looking people milled about aimlessly. Besides the staff everyone wore civilian clothes. To the right of me were two small brown couches and an over-stuffed plaid couch in the center. These couches surrounded a large wooden coffee table. Magazines were fanned out carefully. A few round tables sat empty to the far side of the room; hard plastic chairs placed around them. Towards the back of the room a collection of board games were neatly tucked on a shelf.

A sign above the entrance doors read: *Patients Leaving Must Be Authorized.* The doors were the same ones that I'd wrestled my way through on the way in. I watched a nurse slide her ID through a slot in the door, a buzzing noise followed as she pulled open the door.

Past the main doors was a TV room enclosed in glass with one door to get in and out. The room was small, furnished with a few chairs and a couch facing the TV. The TV was up on a metal rack, out of reach unless you were standing on a chair. Two people sat watching soap operas as they ate. On the door was a big sign that said *No food allowed*.

I followed the doctor and orderly into a brightly lit room. A folded up ping-pong table was tucked to the right of the entrance, an open space to the left, and a sink counter at the far end of the room. An exercise bike and more fold-up chairs were stacked against the wall. The right side of the room featured three large windows and a metal door which led to a roof of sorts. The orderly pulled up chairs and asked me to sit down. The doctor held the clipboard he'd grabbed while walking by the nurses' station earlier. On the clipboard a piece of paper read "Rules and Regulations." The doctor sat down with his chair facing backwards.

I began to fidget.

"Do you know where you are?" The doctor asked.

"I'm not exactly sure." Then I remembered the name of the hospital, "Geisinger, I think."

"That's exactly right, you're on Wing 7 the acute care psychiatric unit at Geisinger Hospital in Danville."

"Why do you call it Wing 7?"

You know I'm not quite sure, It was a name that was carried on from before we moved to this part of the hospital, a little before my time." The doctor spoke a lot like a high school teacher on the first day of class.

"Am I in a nuthouse?" I asked innocently.

"No, it's not a nuthouse, just the wing of an average hospital that fixes people who have brain malfunctions," he said smiling.

"So I'm in a nuthouse?" I repeated.

"Let me start over." Doctor Verrett began a long explanation of what had happened—beginning as far back as my adventures with the rugby club. It started to make a little sense. This marked the first time I'd truly listened to another human since days after arriving to Bloomsburg.

"Intense emotions are common for people suffering from 'bipolar disorder.'" Another first, I'd never heard of this term. "The room you came out of, is sometimes necessary for patients in a manic state. It's the only way we can administer medication and monitor the effects around the clock. It takes time to regulate each person's medication to get the right dosage," he cautioned me. "Every person's different; it depends on how your body reacts. Lithium consists of a natural salt which helps balance the chemicals in the brain that aren't firing correctly. It's as simple as that. Am I making any sense?"

"I guess," I said, but I was a bit lost.

"The most important thing I want you to know about bipolar is that it's a malfunction of the brain, not the mind. Once we regulate the medicine, you'll be as good as new. Lots of people, in fact about two million people, have the same thing you do. Lithium has saved many people's lives," he said, taking a sip of coffee.

Outside of batteries, Lithium was also another name unfamiliar to me.

"You are also taking Tegretol to bring your energy down a notch. That was the blue pill, and the Lithium pills are the smaller, flesh-colored ones. Your intensity level is still extremely high and will remain that way for quite sometime until the medication reaches the best level for you. It's not something you will notice yourself, that's why you're here. We need to monitor how the medication reacts in your system. I've been doing this for twenty years and I can already tell that the Lithium is working. It'll take some time to bring you down to a normal level, but right now you'll be able to concentrate for longer periods of time and your thinking will become clearer every day. Pete, you need to understand that your condition, is serious, but it's also shared by millions of people. A lot of great politicians, actors, writers, and painters have all been through what you're going through. Ted Turner, for example, heads one of the largest corporations in the country, and he has the same disorder. Just make sure you take the medication when the nurse calls your name, follow the rules and you'll be out of here as soon as possible," he said, handing me a booklet on the disorder and a list of notable people in history who lived with bipolar.

When he mentioned, "intelligent, creative, famous people," he got my attention. This was vital to my recovery. It confirmed the belief that I shared a common bond with history's great minds. Those two simple sentences helped me realize that what I had was not a disorder, as much as a side effect of potential greatness. I loved the way the word bipolar sounded. It made me feel like I was in some kind of secret society. Dr. Verrett earned his salary that day and succeeded in reaching me. He simultaneously converted my fear of the unknown into something positive, stroked my ego, and tied taking my medication into getting out of that place.

Today, the hospital wasn't so bad. No one was accusing me of anything. I figured I would be out in a couple of days. The orderly handed me the list of rules. The list said lights out at 9:00 p.m. It also outlined building passes, TV privileges, meal times, exercise schedules, and group meetings. It said that all outgoing phone calls, visitors, and passes would have to be authorized by the doctor.

"When can I make a phone call?" I asked.

"There are no set time frames here. We make our judgments based on the progress that we see. When you are ready, I'll let you know." This was the first time the orderly had spoken.

The doctor stood up and patted me on the back, "You're going to be just fine. Dave will show you around," he continued as the orderly shook my hand. "He's the guy who's gonna be looking out for you here." Having said that, the doctor walked out of the room.

"If you need anything, I'm on duty Tuesday through Saturday, seven in the morning to four in the afternoon. When I'm not around, anyone else can help you. You're going to be here for a while, so I'd better show you around," Dave said.

I looked up at this huge guy and said, "Don't you think they could find me a better-looking nurse?"

"Funny," he replied, walking ahead of me.

The tour brought us to my new room. It looked like most any other hospital room with two beds with a nightstand in between, a dresser along the wall, and a small bathroom to the right of the door. The two bags my mom had brought were on the floor next to one of the beds. I picked one up and searched it. It contained magazines, a few pairs of pants, shirts, underwear, and the usual overnight stuff. The bed next to mine had newspapers and some clothes spread randomly across the neatly made bed.

"Who's my roommate?" I asked Dave.

"Jimmy, ignore him and he won't bother you."

"Sounds like a great roommate, thanks."

"Let me know if you have any problems," Dave stated simply.

"What kind of problems?"

"Nothing in particular, but remember where you are. People here are a little different. If anything happens that you're not comfortable with, let us know immediately."

"No problem," I said, a little puzzled. Looking around I only saw a few old people and a tall skinny guy in the hallway.

"I want a pass as soon as you can get me one," I said eagerly.

"One step at a time," he replied, shaking his head. "Get to know the place first. If you want to get a pass, take it easy and don't break the rules. Got it?"

"Yeah, I think I can handle that."

The shower room was the next stop. Four separate rooms in all two for men two for women. Each one had a combination shower and sink and toilet. There were no locks on the doors only a latch that said "occupied" or "vacant" depending which way you turned it. The mirror was made out of some kind of reflective metal, you could hardly see your face.

"Grab a shower, get dressed and get some food while the cart's still here." Then Dave walked away.

I liked Dave so far. He seemed like a pretty cool dude. Like someone who I could play rugby with. He wasn't bullshitting or talking down to me--just showing me around. I could tell he was proud of this place and that made me feel OK.

The shower was refreshing. The water pressure was strong. I didn't want to get out, but I was hungry. I got dressed in jeans and a white, short-sleeve polo shirt. Gazing at myself in the pseudo-mirror, I noticed that my hair finally was beginning to grow in; I looked like the college student I was supposed to be.

I walked into the main room. Without Dave or the doctor by my side, my previous cocky strut was replaced by a rare display of timidity. Taking a closer look, the other patients resembled aunts and uncles nobody wants to talk to at family parties. The fact that I had something in common with this group frightened me. I didn't see any media moguls or great politicians in this crowd. Dave came from behind the nurses' station and proceeded to introduce me like a teacher would a transfer student. "Everyone please welcome Pete-- he'll be with us for a little while."

A few said hello, others stared silently, some didn't even look up. A funny-looking woman came within a foot of me. I recognized her as the woman who laughed at me when I was first dragged onto Wing 7. She wore way too much makeup, bright blue ballooned-out pants and a shirt with a sparkled rainbow. The strange woman could pass for one of the ladies behind the lunch line at my high school cafeteria. She stopped in front of me and looked up and down, then scurried back to the sofa. Dave stood in the corner overseeing this motley crew.

I hastily grabbed a tray off the food cart. I removed the plastic lid that kept the food warm. The scrambled eggs had a green tint and the toast was soggy, but to me it tasted like a meal from a five-star restaurant.

As the last bite went in my mouth, the funny looking woman who'd run up to me before, sat next to me like she had a secret to tell. She introduced herself nervously as Esmerelda, talking super-fast. I didn't want to be rude so I tried to listen. She rattled off words like a machine gun firing rounds down range. Esmerelda fascinated me.

The story she told involved mysterious forces which compelled her to kill her fuzzy hamster named Kid. Apparently mysterious forces made this nice lady kill Kid, her only friend in the cruel world. Then they took her far down a country road, where she had to bury the poor, dead rodent in a secret location.

I got up and put my tray into the slot like everyone else had. I stopped and asked Dave, "What's the deal with Esmerlelda?"

"Her name is Betty and she has what's known as schizophrenia." He replied.

"Don't worry Pete, her disorder is completely different than what you have," he finished.

"Did she kill her hamster?" I asked.

He looked at me like he didn't know what I was talking about and he turned to go back behind the plexiglas.

In my tempered manic state, I had an unexplainable way of deciphering the meaning behind Esmeralda's disjointed tale. Behind the words, her eyes told me the real story. She was trying to get across a message. "Hey, you, new guy, I am totally confused. I used to be a normal person and something went terribly wrong along the way, can you help?"

At eleven we were supposed to have a group meeting, it was ten. I didn't know what to do until then. Everyone seemed to wander around in his or her own world. I made my way to a window sill in the main area. I moved the heavy curtains to the side and saw the gorgeous day I was missing. To my right two gigantic red maple trees cast a partial shadow over a man made pond. Over to the left I watched a man walk across a parking lot to his car, get in, and drive away. I turned around and studied my new surroundings. It looked to me like I was the only patient under thirty. Wing 7 had a sterile smell and lonely nursing home feel. A flash sensation of claustrophobia and nausea overwhelmed me. I wanted to make a brake for the door. I remembered the padded room and had second thoughts.

Eventually, I sat down and read a *Newsweek* magazine. My concentration level wouldn't allow me past the first paragraph. Instead I tried to figure out how each of these people ended up here.

I named one guy Marathon Man because he never stopped pacing the hallways. From the look of his hair, he might have the same stylist as Charlie Manson. Unlike Charlie, he had an innocent look. His journey up and down the halls was relentless. He did a military style about-face at an invisible line just before he reached the main room. The repeated actions mesmerized me. His physical comedy cracked me up. On the other hand, I felt sorry for him.

In the TV room sat a lady who never moved an inch. I could only see her from a side angle. Her dark, bushy, curly hair and dark complexion made me think she might be from the Middle East. She was staring up at the TV but it wasn't on. She did not make a single motion the entire time I watched her. Her frozen posture reminded me of a store mannequin. I dubbed her the Statue Lady.

I looked down at the paper that the doctor had given me and remembered that the group meeting was to start in a few minutes. Two orderlies came from behind the Plexiglas counter, walked up to each person in the room and asked if they'd join the meeting. There were about ten people around the room and seven of us made our way over to the couches and chairs that had been pulled up.

A young nurse tried to get everyone's attention as she began the meeting. She wore the same white pants and shirt with blue edges, her nametag read Janet Zubroski. Janet had bright red hair and a nervous smile. She couldn't have been more than a year or two older than me. The look on her face said, "I want to help everybody, but I haven't the slightest clue how to do it."

I felt green, as if it were my first day on a new job. Esmerelda, aka Hamster Lady, was on one end of the couch. On the opposite end sat the Statue Lady. In between was a guy who seemed jittery. Two other nurses joined in after a few minutes. A monstrously large man, wearing painter pants and a stained t-shirt, sat next to one of the nurses. His Neanderthal-sloping forehead and blank stare sent a quick shiver down my spine. He didn't seem to interact with anyone and appeared agitated. He reminded me of what I've always pictured *Lenny* from *Of Mice and Men* to look like. Marathon Man continued to go for the world's record in long-distance hall pacing.

In sharp contrast to the guy pacing the halls was an older silver haired man who walked excruciatingly slowly towards the couches. His neatly-pressed flannel shirt was tucked into corduroy pants and he sported a pair of shined cordovan loafers. The old-timer showed a feisty side when he pushed the nurse's hand away as she guided him to his seat. I imagined him as some sort of godfather to this peculiar group.

"Jack, we're glad you joined us," the nurse said warmly. Seated in a plastic chair, he smiled. I couldn't tell if his smile was fake or genuine. Patients like Jack, Marathon Man, and Esmerlelda stood out. Others seemed to blend into the background like furniture.

The meeting started with typical classroom-style introductions. The young nurse's voice trembled; she spoke as if she was a substitute teacher addressing a class of school children.

Janet went around and asked each person to introduce themselves. Everyone except me knew the drill. The Statue Lady said in a dull, almost mouse-like tone that her name was Kate. She looked down after speaking and didn't say anything else.

"Sam, can you say hello to the group today?"

His big round eyeballs drifted to the side as he just looked at her without saying a word.

"Okay, well, everyone this is Sam. He's from Berwick," she said, pointing to him.

Janet went around the room until she finally got to me. I wanted to tell my life story. I began by saying my full name, Peter Dameon Dagit Barnes. I explained that my original name was Peter Dameon Barnes, but my mother had legally changed my middle name to Dagit when my parents had separated. "I just put one D down when I sign my name. I like both names, Dameon because it's a cool name and Dagit because it's a family name." Then I rambled on about being from the suburbs of Philadelphia. I could have kept going all day.

Janet cut me off ever so graciously. I was just getting started and was not happy, but since I was the new kid on the block, I conceded and let her move on. I gathered she understood how intelligent I was, and so I didn't cast too hard of a judgment on her. I assumed she was playing to the lowest common denominator.

Next, Janet asked Jack to introduce himself. He flashed a huge grin then hocked up as much phlegm as he possibly could and spit it into a plastic cup, "Jack's my name, Bloomsburg born and raised." Then he looked back up with a smile and didn't say another word. Janet ignored the spitting and flashed back a frown. Everyone was snickering but seemed afraid to laugh, except for Esmerelda, who burst out laughing and continued to occasionally erupt into laughter throughout the rest of the meeting. I didn't know what to make of the situation. Despite my feelings of unease, this place kept my attention.

CHAPTER SEVEN

Day Twenty Two continued: Arts & Crafts

September 22, 1989

Today's highlight was Arts and Crafts. I was curious as hell to see what kind of Arts and Crafts these guys would come up with. As the group broke up, I thanked Janet for a wonderful meeting. I was fairly certain the nurses were fighting over who would get to date me first when I got out of here.

I picked up a local newspaper and scanned through. Before I set the paper down, an advertisement caught my eye. Big and bold the ad showed college kids on the beach and said, *Spring Break for Free!*

"Peter, put the paper away. It's time to go downstairs," Nurse Janet said as she rounded people up for Arts and Crafts.

"Wow, this is the way to go!" I said out loud and pointed to the ad.

The gist of the ad was that if you got ten or more students to book a vacation through this company, you could go for free. If you booked more people you would get a cash bonus based on the total number of people who went on the trip. Earn money, get your friends a deal, and go on vacation! What a brilliant idea. The advertisement sent my semi-manic mind into a frenzy. How easy could it be? There were thousands of kids at Bloomsburg; I could get at least a hundred. Here was a spark--another brilliant idea that was bound to catapult me into instant wealth. I saved the ad for later use.

As I got up from the couch, I looked over and saw a young girl at the nurses' station who looked to be around my age. She had an "I can't believe I'm in a freaking mental hospital" look on her face. The blue and white Penn State t-shirt that she wore was too big. Her jeans were faded with a patch sewn into the area covering her left knee. She had long brown hair that went halfway down her back. I was excited to see the nurse bring her into the Arts and Crafts lineup. I wondered if she was bipolar too.

Extra care was taken to ensure that we made it down to the art classroom without incident. We were lined up in the main room. Two nurses and two male orderlies flanked the group. The orderlies took up the rear and the females positioned themselves on the side. We separated into groups and took two different elevators to the basement. We walked down what seemed like endless corridors of white walled brick hallways. Every once in a while I couldn't help but jump up and touch the top brick. We made it to a room that resembled a kindergarten room decorated by hippies. A strong odor of Elmer's glue and paint penetrated my nostrils. The walls were painted with bright colors and a rainbow on the far wall. Painted beads, collages and other junk were scattered around the room. Circular carpets covered the floor along with almost child-size tables and chairs.

I waited and tried to position myself next to the new girl who had taken the second elevator. She walked by and I asked if she wanted a seat. She sat down looking at me but not saying anything. The chairs were awkward hard plastic seats with curved metal legs. The chairs were small, but because I'm short, they didn't bother me. On the other hand, Sam, the Neanderthal guy, had a hard time getting comfortable in the miniature chair. He sat across the table from me, and I had to hold back my laughter as he squirmed and cursed under his breath.

The nurse began to list the rules of the room.

"Welcome to Wing 7, the human terrarium," I said to the girl sitting next to me. It sounded corny when it came out.

"Thanks," she said without looking up.

"Do you go to Penn State?" I asked.

She smiled and finally looked at me. "I hate Penn State. I just borrowed this t-shirt." I'd never seen green eyes like hers, they reminded me of emeralds.

I told her my name was Pete and put my hand out. I didn't expect her firm grip. "Well, hello Pete," she said sarcastically.

"Do you have a name?"

"Sorry, it's Sara."

"Cool name," I said, again sounding like an idiot.

As time passed, she began to warm up to me and we were joking around with each other. She was small but she had a tough presence about her. When a smile did finally cross her face, she looked like a completely different person. She was naturally beautiful.

Sara told me she was seventeen and starting her junior year in high school. It turned out that she was not the ordinary nut-job like everyone else.

"How come you're in here? You're crazy, too?" I asked.

"No, it's 'cause my Mom's a fucking junkie bitch, that's why," she said showing me a huge bruise on her arm.

"No way! Your mom did that?" I examined her arm.

"I'm just here until my best friend's parents can legally get custody of me. I'm moving with her family to Arizona. I can't wait to get away from this town anyway." she said angrily.

"She beats you?"

"I'm sorry I brought it up. I don't feel like getting into it right now," Sara said without much emotion.

"Man that sucks," I said. "When I was sixteen my father and I used to get in fights all the time when he was drinking. We moved away from him when I was sixteen."

"Yeah, well my mom and her asshole boyfriend can kiss my ass." Sara started fumbling with a paint brush.

I dropped the subject. I didn't want to piss off the only friend I had made. I was ready to let her in on my new plan to build a business empire. I whispered as if someone might steal my idea, "How would you like to be in Cancun, Mexico right now?"

Sara quickly changed the subject. She turned her head to make sure no one was listening. "You know, this place is strange."

"I've noticed," I said as if I wasn't included in her assessment.

It wasn't the place that was strange, rather the artisans who were mutilating even the most elementary of Arts and Crafts projects. Kate, the Statue Lady, was in the corner staring at the pile of Popsicle sticks in front of her. The nurse in charge made a valiant effort but gave up after repeated attempts to inspire her. Kate's only response was an occasional upward glance that seemed to say, 'thanks but leave me alone.'

The Hamster Lady, however, was working feverishly at what had to be the coolest finger painting I had ever seen. She walked around the room showing off her masterpiece, rambling on about correlations between the artwork and her hamster. There was no similarity whatsoever to a rodent, or anything else for that matter. A classic finger-painting yes, a hamster it certainly wasn't.

The others were peacefully talking to themselves, or rocking back and forth on their chairs nervously. Reflecting upon myself, I think I had been doing a little rocking myself. If you stepped back, the whole room looked like a super-sized kindergarten class.

I felt Sam was eyeing my every move. Sara noticed it too.

"What's his deal?" Sara asked.

"I have no idea, but I wouldn't want him on my bad side," I responded quietly.

"He seems weird."

"Yeah and…? Look where we are." We both laughed.

As Arts and Crafts ended, we all washed off our brushes, placed the lids back on the glue jars, and put all the supplies back in their original place. Back to Wing 7 we went. By now I was feeling right at home.

The lunch cart rolled in and I was starving again. Despite the plastic aftertaste, the food was decent. If appetite was any indication of recovery, I was well on my way. I sat with Kate, the Statue Lady, and Sara. Of course, I did all the talking, which was fine by them. Kate barely ate anything. "Are you going to eat that chocolate pudding," I asked her. Kate's typical brooding look became warm and she almost smiled when she pushed her pudding my way.

"Why are you so depressed?" I asked bluntly.

She fought it but a smile burst across her face. "When you've eaten this food for over a week, you'll be depressed, too," she said so softly I could hardly hear her. When I did figure out what she'd said, her sense of humor totally took me by surprise.

Meanwhile, back on the farm, Marathon Man was going full speed up and down the hallway. I asked Kate and Sara what they thought of him.

"He does that all day, every day," Kate said.

Sara was giggling, "How can he keep it up?" After we finished the meal, my curiosity got the best of me. I began to pace right alongside him. I had to jog to keep up.

"Hey what's the deal?" I said with genuine interest. He didn't even look my way. He kept right on marching.

"You're better at this than most of the guys in basic training. Can you do push-ups?"

No reaction. Sara and Kate were looking at me as if I was a four-year-old.

Dave grabbed my arm. "Pete, knock it off," he said in a harsh whisper.

"I was just trying to help," I said, pulling my arm back.

"Remember, this ain't a game, it's not college. He's not like most of the other people in here; he's chronic--like a paraplegic. The more crap like that you pull, the longer you'll have to stay. A few days ago we all could have made fun of you. You're a smart kid--use your head."

He was right. Now I felt like a jerk. I decided to go back to my room where I was lucky enough to meet Jimmy. He was a weasel of a man with a receding hairline, dark eyes, a large forehead, and thin arms. He was the kind of low life guy Mulder and Scully of the *X Files* would be interviewing after somebody was abducted. I don't scare easily, but this guy gave off strange vibes from the moment I saw him.

"Hey, how's it going?" I ventured.

He kept right along with what he was doing.

"How's it going?" I said louder.

"Who the fuck are you, another doctor? Who sent you?" he said, jerking his head up with an accusing glance.

"I'm no doctor, I'm your roommate,"

"This is my side. Don't cross the line!" he growled.

"Don't worry asshole, I won't," I mumbled under my breath.

He kept moving around as he talked.

"Asshole? Do you know who you're talking to? Do you know what's going on? You better figure it out quick, because it's all around, and you're a part of it!"

"Sorry, man. I didn't mean anything by it," I said to try and calm him down.

"Just keep talking, keep talk talk talk talking," he said, mocking me in a chicken voice. "I can kill you in two seconds, nobody will even care. As a matter of fact…" He waved his hands around like a retarded karate fighter. "Ha!" he yelled. "Your fucking soul is mine now, motherfucker! You mortals have no clue what's coming, do you?" He stood staring directly at me.

Then with a shaky and trembling voice he said, "Well, do you?"

He looked like he needed a cigarette real bad. His tone changed from a rant to an eerie calm. Jimmy bugged me out. I grabbed my books and walked back to the main area.

I went to look for Dave to see if I could change rooms, but he had just left. Trying to forget my roommate situation, I flipped the pictures in my art history book. There was a note inside the book from one of my teachers. It listed all of my subjects and the pages I needed to read in each book. At the bottom she wrote: "Pete, these are the chapters you will need to know when you come back. Good luck with your recovery. Everybody hopes you return soon," signed, "Ms. Shari Kiehnbaum, Student Advisor."

This was amazing news! I didn't even know I had a student advisor. It didn't take long to forget about my roommate. All I could think about was sitting in class with other students my age.

After a few minutes, the small window at the nurses' station opened and a nurse I hadn't seen before said in a cheery tone, "It's time for meds." I approached the window and Kate followed slowly behind me. There were only two speeds in this place, fast-forward and slow motion. Each little cup had a name on it, and it looked like the nurses spent half the morning arranging this amazing array of colors and combinations. I couldn't help but think of Grace Slick and her deep voice singing "One pill makes you larger, one pill makes you small… Go ask Alice, when she's ten feet tall."

This was the first time I had the choice to get up and go get my medicine rather than have someone feed it to me as part of a meal or to get me to agree to something. I didn't mind. I trusted Dave and Dr. Verrett. So far, the medication seemed to be working, and I didn't want to end up like Marathon Man. I downed the pills and smiled, waiting for approval. I wanted to get on the good side of the nurses so they would tell Dave I deserved a pass. The nurse in charge of my dose said, "Good job!" Sara was the only one who didn't have to take any medication. I think she secretly felt a little left out.

That night at dinner, Sara, Kate, Esmerelda, Jack, one of the female night nurses, and I sat at one of the large, round tables. Jack asked everyone to say grace. When he folded his hands to pray, I noticed his unusually long fingernails that were stained yellow. I tried to picture him at my age. Did he play sports? Was he good with the ladies? I never associated myself with the rest of these people. I was only a visitor passing through. I hoped to whatever god was out there that I would not ever end up in a place like this at his age.

I went along with the prayer despite my lack of faith. If it made Jack happy, that was good enough for me.

"Bless us, oh Lord, and these thy gifts which we are about to receive, from thy bounty through Christ, our Lord, Amen," Jack said.

After Jack said "Amen," Esmerelda clapped her hands three times over her head.

Jack opened his eyes, gave a grandfatherly smile and said, "Dig in." Then, he examined each piece of meal with his fork; like a paleontologist sifting through ancient dinosaur remains.

We ate without saying much. Jack was talking calmly to a nurse, when all of a sudden he looked at me as if I had never been at the table before. He clenched his plastic utensils like weapons, breaking the fork in half. His face filled with rage and he began to scream.

"Drug dealer! You're the goddamn dealer that killed my son! Get that son of a bitch out of here! What the hell is he doing here?" he said in a high-pitched tone.

"Drug dealer? What's he talking about?" I said, looking around for support.

The nurse tried to calm him down, but he only got worse.

"I've never sold drugs in my life. I don't even know where to buy a bag of pot in this town," I explained.

"FUCKING SCUM!!!!!!!" Jack was spitting as he yelled. Orderlies rushed over to make sure things didn't get out of hand.

"Hey, I'm sorry about your son, but I never knew him," I said.

"It's not you. He does this sometimes. He's schizophrenic," the nurse said as she held him back.

This only made him more agitated. "He killed my boy. Get him out of here," Jack cried out. Then as fast as he had gone into the fit, he calmed down. He acted as if nothing had happened.

"Pete, it has nothing to do with you," a nurse said, trying to reassure me.

The rest of the meal went by without incident. Later on the nurse told me Jack had never been married and didn't have a son. This place got stranger and stranger every minute.

That night Sara and I sat next to each other, watching TV for a while. We quickly discovered that we had a similar hatred for most eighties music. We were practicing self-torture by watching MTV. Sara got up and started mocking the latest Milli Vanilli video.

"Girl you know it's true!" she sang and danced around the room. Then she screamed, "It makes me want to puke!"

She cracked me up. A brief feeling of "normal" hit me. We sat close and our arms kept brushing up against each other. I could tell she liked me. The fact that we were in a mental ward became the furthest thing from our minds. For me, the manic state was like being on a love drug. My sense of touch and sexuality was heightened dramatically. It wasn't only sex that I desired, but I craved physical touch and admiration from others. But I held back my desire to grab her and kiss her. Good thing because we were drawing stares from the peanut gallery of nurses.

Sara sat on the couch and crossed her legs. "Do you want to know the real reason I ended up here?" she asked shyly.

"I thought your mom hit you?"

"She's hit me plenty of times, but that's not all of it," she looked down.

"What then?"

"The part about moving to Arizona and my mom being a bitch, that's all true, it's just not everything; I'm afraid I'll sound like some kind of stupid slut."

"Slut, what are you talking about?"

"Promise you won't hate me if I tell you?"

"Hate you, are you kidding?" I said.

Staring at the ground Sara shared her story. "My real dad died when my mom was pregnant with me."

"Oh man, I'm sorry," I said.

"He was drunk and he drove off the road. He was nineteen and my mom was eighteen. After he died my mom started taking drugs and she was with different guys all the time. My mom's boyfriends have all been assholes, every freaking one." She paused. "When I was ten, her boyfriend was a schoolteacher--a fucking gym teacher who sold coke." She laughed nervously. "He took me to a playground and made me watch him play with his dick." She stopped again. "I was so confused, when I finally told my mom, she slapped me in the face and told me I was lying. She always blames me for her inability to find a good man."

Sara looked at me with tears in her eyes. "I'm sorry to tell you all this, I know it's fucked-up shit. I've never told anyone this besides my friend Lori."

"I promise it's fine," I said, squeezing her hand.

"I just need you to understand the kind of bitch she is. She's the one that should be in here."

She put her head on my shoulder.

"Last weekend my mom went to stay with her cousins in Hazelton. Dale, her latest ass-face boyfriend is barely twenty-one. He's living off a bullshit workman's comp because of a bad back, but he plays football with his friends every weekend," she said, rolling her eyes. "Friday, Dale bought a bag of pot and a case of beer and told me to invite some friends over. A couple people came over and we all got pretty wasted. About three in the morning, my friends left and I passed out on the couch watching TV. I woke without any pants on. Dale was completely naked trying to climb on top of me. Still half asleep I kicked him as hard as I could in the face. You should have seen his skinny drunk ass lying on the ground; I have never seen a smaller . . ." She stopped herself and almost laughed. "I knew he had a gun somewhere in the house, so I ran out the front door. It wasn't till the cold air hit me that I remembered I was half naked. I kept running until I made it to Lori's house. I snuck in the back door and went to her room. I was so dizzy; I puked all over her carpet."

"Unbelievable." I was taken back.

"Lori never told her parents, but Dale, the idiot, had the balls to call Lori's dad and say he was going to kill me. Her dad called the police and got his ass arrested."

"The next day my mom posted bail for the jerk. Dumb ass Dale told my mom I'd made everything up to break 'em up. The fucking bitch believed him over me!

"That sucks," was all I could say. Growing up in an alcoholic family I'd seen my share of screwed up things, but I'd never heard this kind of story before.

"The cops put me in here because they said it's the only place they could make sure I was safe while Lori's parents filed for custody," she said, pulling her head from my shoulder and sitting up.

A nurse walked in the TV room.

"Sara, is everything okay?" the nurse asked.

"Yeah, I'm cool. We're just talking."

"Well, it's time for you guys to head to bed." The nurse held the door open and waited for us to leave.

"Listen, it's going to get better. It's good you're getting the hell away from your mom," I said, getting up.

"You're the nicest guy," Sara said, wrapping her arms around me in a bear hug and kissing my cheek.

My face turned bright red as we both headed for our rooms. As I opened the door to my room, I remembered Jimmy. I hoped he was already asleep. Knowing that the nurses and orderlies were on duty 24/7 was my only comfort.

I wasn't tired in the slightest. Trying not to wake up Jimmy, I crept into my bed. A small crack in the curtain allowed enough streetlight into the room to see outlines. He appeared to be asleep. As I rolled over, the bed made an obnoxiously loud, creaking noise.

"Who's there?" I heard him whisper. "Who's in my room goddamn-it?" I didn't answer. Then I heard the pull of the metal cord of the lamp in between our beds. Bam! The light came on, nearly blinding me.

"Yo, man, I'm trying to get some sleep," I said, rolling over.

"Bullshit, you woke up my ass, now you're staying up until I say. You don't know shit, do you? I only have one question, are you with me?" Jimmy said, as if I knew exactly what he was talking about. In a way, his weird questions and peculiar voice sparked my interest. At one point, he put his face about two inches from mine, trying to scare me. His breath was rank. As he began to go into another rant, an orderly doing rounds heard him talking. Our door opened.

"Get to sleep. Jimmy, you know the drill. Don't bug the new guy," the orderly said, shining his flashlight in the room. I thought that would be the end of that and I could at least try to sleep.

"Fuck off and mind your own business or I'll stick that flashlight up your ass, big boy," Jimmy laughed.

"Watch your mouth Jimmy, this is a family place, just don't make me come back." the orderly said, shaking his head as he turned out the light.

"Whatever, mortal," Jimmy sounded like a child.

The moment the night orderly left, Jimmy talked about how evil permeated everywhere. He bragged that he was responsible for the deaths of hundreds of people. He claimed that the more people he murdered on earth, the more power he would have in the afterlife.

"Taking the souls of babies gives you the most power," he said again, getting too close for my comfort.

"You can join us or become one of our sacrifices." Each time he approached my fists clinched. As he spoke, he spit and made wild gestures with his hands.

"If you've never tasted warm blood, then you won't have a chance in the afterlife," he said, laughing out loud. Jimmy seemed to be in a trance.

"Here, look. You want proof!" he said angrily.

He turned on the light again, grabbed some papers from his drawer, and slapped them on the nightstand in between our beds.

"No, it's cool. I believe you." I moved away.

He showed me black and white sketches of a barn, with a huge alter in the center, drawings of people with limbs cut off and pages full of names.

"I killed every one of these idiots," he said, slamming his hand down on a page with a list of names.

He freaked me out. I couldn't fall asleep.

Eventually natural light came through the cracks of the curtains. The new shade of light revealed that Jimmy looked worn out--he even seemed a bit scared of himself. All I wanted to do was leave the room, but he kept pacing between my bed and the door most of the time. My glowing watch read 4:30 a.m.

When Jimmy went to use the bathroom, I made a break for it. I walked out of the room and down the hall as fast as I could while trying not to draw any attention. At the end of the hall, I found a nurse. She was an older, hefty lady, with a trashy romance novel plastered up against her pudgy face. When I got closer she looked at me as if to say, kid, you'd better be bleeding profusely.

"Go back to bed. There are two hours before breakfast," she said, pulling the book down to her nose.

"I'm not tired. I won't cause any trouble, I promise." I said.

She shook her head and went on reading, "Okay, just be quiet."

I sat down and pretended to read magazines until breakfast. As long as I wasn't in the same room as Jimmy, I was happy.

CHAPTER EIGHT

Day Twenty Three: Adjusting To "Wing 7"

September 23, 1989

An hour went by before anyone else stirred. Kate was the first to begin to wander down the hallway. She was wearing a bulky, yellow robe. From a distance, Kate looked eighty years old. In reality, she was probably in her mid-thirties. She slumped over and dragged her feet. Her hair was a big ball of curls, having no general direction other then outward. I stared as she crept inch by inch. I wanted to yell, "Come on, you can do it, you can do it!" But the past five hours of hell with Jimmy had me shaken.

Kate sat down on the couch in the TV room. I poked my head around the door and said good morning. She looked up, and returned the greeting with a half wave. I wanted to see if she knew anything about my roommate.

"Do you have a second?" I asked.

Before she could answer, I began to tell her everything I could remember about what spewed from Jimmy's mouth.

"I'm barely awake, Pete. Calm down. I can't understand you," Kate interrupted.

My effort to describe the horrors of my first night on the wing was more amusing than frightening. She put the back of her hand on her mouth, and smiled. "Oh Pete, that guy's all talk. He's had three roommates since I got here."

She made me feel gullible for believing him. I dropped the whole thing so I wouldn't sound so stupid.

Dave walked in the room, "I hear you were making a lot of noise last night."

"Me? I didn't do anything!" I said.

Dave laughed. "I'm sorry, I was afraid that might happen. He's been good for a couple days. Don't worry, Jimmy's being transferred to Hazelton. It's closer to his home. His wife will pick him up today. Lithium doesn't work for him, and it takes a lot of time for some people to find the right medication. Jimmy's actually a nice guy when he's not manic.

"He has the same thing I do?" I said astonished.

"Well, everyone's different; Jimmy went a long time without getting any help."

"But he has bipolar?" I asked.

"Yep," he said, filling out paperwork.

"Man, that's messed up." I couldn't believe it.

"Hey, go chill for a few minutes. When I finish this paperwork, I have a job for you," Dave said, opening the door to the staff room.

"A job, what kind of job?" I asked, but he disappeared.

I tried to envision how Jimmy and I could have anything in common.

Dave reappeared, "You're in luck, you'll have the room to yourself until we figure something out,"

"Oh that's cool," I said, still thinking about my roommate.

"I've got something you can help me with. Maybe we can burn off some of that energy."

I followed Dave into the room as he introduced me to Nurse Nancy.

"Hi! How are you feeling today?" she said like a cheerleader warming up a crowd. Her high-pitched voice could have melted paint. Nurse Nancy had big Bon Jovi hair and purple leg warmers that she wore over her white nurse's pants. She wrangled up the rest of the cast of characters while Dave and I moved chairs to create a makeshift aerobic studio. I went to find Kate who was still sitting on the couch.

156

"No way," was her first response.

"Come on, it will be good for you," I said.

Then I did what any polite teenager would do, and dragged her up by the arm.

"I'll go watch, but only because I know you won't stop bugging me."

Nurse Nancy plugged in her portable tape deck and Paula Abdul's latest song, *Straight Up*, got the party started, well sort of.

"How's everyone feeling?" the bubbly nurse yelled.

From the back, Jack yelled out, "I feel like dog crap!"

We started with a simple stretch.

"Touch your toes!" then "Reach for the sky, come on, you can reach higher than that! Now everybody wiggle." She started moving her hips. She looked comical, but not as funny as the rest of us.

We progressed to running in place to the beat of Tina Turner singing *Proud Mary*. Esmerelda stood in place and picked her nose. I was so pumped; I stepped right next to Nurse Nancy and began calling out an army cadence and stomping my feet to the rhythm.

"They say that in the army, the coffee's mighty fine,
It looks like muddy water, and tastes like turpentine!

Sound off, one two, sound off three four..."

No one seemed to understand, but I didn't care. Jack was now shadow boxing. Kate had her hands over her face while shaking her head, embarrassed for me. This scene was a Richard Simmons video gone wrong.

Dave let me stay up front for a minute, then he came over and told me to get back in the group. Nurse Nancy ended the class. "Remember everybody, love life and it will love you back!" she said out of breath.

Exercise class was held every day. The time was a great way to release my pent-up energy.

As we walked back into the main room, I noticed a guy who looked even younger than Sara and me being escorted quietly through the double doors. He wore a green hospital shirt, blue jeans, and scruffy long blonde hair. Headphones hung around his neck. He was one of the skinniest people I've ever seen. Our whole group of aerobicising mental patients stared at the latest addition to Wing 7 as we walked back through the main room. He looked in our direction but never made eye contact with anyone.

"Who's the new guy?" Sara whispered in my ear from behind.

"Shit, you scared me. I don't know. He just came in. Hey, how did you get out of exercise class?"

"I slept through most of it, but I caught you guys as I was going to the shower. Pretty amusing, I must say."

"You better come tomorrow. I'm gonna take a shower, save me a seat when breakfast comes."

As I walked away she said with a flirtatious smile, "Hey Jane Fonda, you looked kind of cute doing your exercises."

"Oh make fun of the mental patient, that's real cool." I joked walking away.

I nearly had a head-on collision with Marathon Man when I turned the corner. He didn't even flinch as I swerved out of his way. My heart raced as I thought about Sara. I couldn't believe I was in a mental facility and a cute girl was flirting me.

I ducked into my room. Jimmy wasn't there. He must have left while we were exercising. I breathed a sigh of relief, grabbed some clothes and hit the shower, then made my way to breakfast with lightning speed. It felt like summer camp. All the anxiety of getting there was over and I had made a couple of friends.

I sat with Sara and Kate eventually joined us. We were becoming quite comfortable in each other's company. An odd match, but we got along well.

"Why are you here?" Sara asked Kate.

"They call it postpartum depression," she said openly.

"How long before you get better?" I asked.

"I've been on this wing a week and the doctor said I might be here a few more." Kate spoke softly like the female version of the Marlon Brandow; I had to lean in to hear her.

"Weeks?" I asked surprised.

"Yeah, but I'm not leaving until I feel the way I used to." Her voice rose a notch.

"About five months ago, I had a beautiful baby boy born here in this hospital. His name is Jacob, he's my angel," Kate continued.

"That's great!" I broke in awkwardly.

"He's our only child. Neil, my husband, is taking care of him now. I miss them both so much."

After a long pause, she cleared her throat and continued.

"After Jacob's birth strange things started happening to me. Sometimes I couldn't remember Jacob's name. I would try so hard, but nothing came to me. I called Neil's office and screamed at his secretary to get him. I'm so embarrassed."

"Jacob caught a mild fever a month after he was born. That's when I lost it. I started sterilizing every part of the house. Once I finished, I started all over again. I was deathly tired, but I couldn't stop. A lot of times, I got so busy cleaning I'd forget to feed Jacob. Neil came home last week, he found me on the kitchen floor scrubbing, completely naked. I thought my clothes had been contaminated with germs and might kill the baby.

"Neil's an economics professor at Bloomsburg, he called a friend in the psychology department. His friend practically diagnosed my situation over the phone. Neil brought me here the next day."

"Believe it or not, I'm a hundred times better than I was two weeks ago. Neil's bringing Jacob in as soon as the doctor says its okay." Kate spoke with more animation in her voice.

"That's cool, I can't wait to meet them," Sara said after sipping her cup of coffee.

Before I entered Wing 7, I had no idea how many types of mental illnesses there were and how people were treated. News stories about serial killers and the occasional horror movie were my only exposure to the topic. There was a great deal I did not know.

A nurse ran over to stop Esmerelda from throwing her scrambled eggs. I was munching away on some kind of rock-hard muffin as the new guy passed by on his grand tour. Dave and a doctor I hadn't seen before were escorting him.

After the tour, Dave brought him over to our table.

"Hey everyone, this is Damian." Dave introduced Damian exactly the way he did with me.

Dave looked at me. "It looks like we found you a roommate."

I was happy to have someone closer to my age and quite frankly anyone who wasn't Jimmy. Damian sat down without a word. He looked a little scared and his eyes were bloodshot.

Sara asked him if he wanted some orange juice. "Sure, thanks," he answered shyly. Reaching for the glass, his sleeve pulled back and revealed a brand-new bandage over his wrist.

He pulled his arm back quickly.

"What happened to your arm?" I asked innocently.

"Oh, yeah. I cut myself," he said, and then looked down abruptly.

He didn't say anything else after that. Sara and Kate looked embarrassed as I asked my stupid question. It didn't cross my mind that, just a day before, doctors were working feverishly in the emergency room to sew up his arm after an attempted suicide. Sara quickly changed the subject.

"So where are you from?" she asked Damian.

"I go to Bloomsburg High School," he replied, still looking down.

She told him that she was from Danville. They traded names of kids she knew from Bloomsburg. It seemed to break the tension and put everyone at ease. I could tell Damian was a good person.

The next major event of the day was the group meeting. Janet, the same nurse from the day before, began rallying the troops. I made sure to get a seat on the couch. Sara sat across from me. A short nurse on the other side of the room looked like a miniature person standing next to Sam, as she tried to convince him how fun the meeting would be. Janet guided Sam to the couch and he sat next to Sara. She smiled back and looked at me as if to say, "Please, help." The Hamster Lady sat down next to me and began to rattle off more nonsense. Damian came back and I introduced him to the Hamster Lady as the lovely and talented Esmerelda. I motioned for him to sit next to her, and he looked a little pissed. I told Esmerelda that Damian was the newest addition to the terrarium. Not everyone thought the human terrarium line was as funny as I thought it was. She had no idea what I was talking about. Jack was on the opposite couch next to Sara and Sam. He acted as if he had never met any of us before. He smiled and then frowned, smiled then frowned, again.

The nurse called my name from her chart. I looked up and it seemed everyone had already rattled off his or her histories. This time I spared the nurse and kept my introduction brief.

Looking over at Damian, the nurse asked, "Could you tell the group your name and where you are from?" I wondered if she ever realized she was speaking baby talk.

"Well, I'm Damian, I'm sixteen, and I go to Bloomsburg High School," he stated.

"Welcome, Damian. It's good to have you here," the nurse said.

At the end of the meeting, the nurse announced we were all going outside. The plan was to go on a nature walk around the hospital to a nearby natural water spring. Once a week, the nurses took the patients for a walk around the hospital grounds if the weather was nice. This meant we actually got to go outside.

We lined up as we had the day before to go to the Arts and Crafts room. This time, the security presence was more visible. Three orderlies, including Dave, went with us. Two groups went down the elevator and landed at the main lobby. Bystanders watched us pile off the elevator like clowns getting out of a Volkswagen. I was out in front with Sara and Esmerelda not far behind. Sam, Jack, and some others followed. Damian and Kate brought up the rear.

When we got outside I put my arms up in the air as if I'd just crossed a finish line. The sun and crisp air blew me away. I was so alive. I breathed the crisp September air as if for the first time. Grabbing Sara, I twirled her around.

Our group continued our walk around the building, then down a nature path in the woods, next to the hospital. We wound up at a wall of boulders that had a pipe with water pouring out. The nurses had brought some empty jugs and plastic cups. We filled them up and everyone took a drink. This was the first time I'd ever drunk water from a natural spring. It tasted incredible. Eventually, we made a circle around the hospital then headed for the elevators. We carried the plastic containers back to Wing 7 and completed our mission by pouring the spring water into the main cooler.

Later that night, Wing 7 quieted down. Sara, Kate, Damian and I monopolized the TV room. I hadn't watched TV for so long that I didn't have a clue as to what was on. Sara grabbed the TV Guide and flipped through it. I took the remote and flicked on the TV. Sara listed our choices. *Perfect Strangers, Family Matters, Erkle, Cops, Dallas,* and the premiere of a show called *Baywatch.*

"The *Baywatch* show sounds OK," Damian said faintly.

"Ewh, that's the new show about those girls with huge tits running down the beach. I don't want to watch that," Sara whined.

Just then the theme song for *Baywatch* came on and the decision was made. The ladies feigned boredom, but the good-looking, tan-bodied men on the show didn't hurt our cause.

As the slow music played in the background, all you could see were huge breasts bouncing up and down the beach, garnished by a life preserver. Then David Hasselhoff, the guy from *Night Rider,* jogged in slow motion down the beach. He looked so out of place we couldn't help but laugh. After the opening scene, we lost interest in the show, and the conversation moved from casual to serious. Sara turned to Damian and asked, "So, how did you cut yourself?"

After how she had cut me off at breakfast her question surprised me.

165

"Well, it's actually my second time here," Damian pulled up his sleeves. One wrist was scarred, the other patched with a fresh bandage.

"I am so sorry. You don't have to say anything. I was just curious," Sara apologized.

"It's fine. I was fucking stupid," he said, looking up.

Despite the abrupt way Sara had questioned him, we could tell Damian was not offended. Sometimes it's easier to talk with fellow patients than doctors and nurses. He was so young, even compared to me, and it showed. He seemed to enjoy describing how his three-day stint in the emergency room began when his parents found him lying in a pool of blood hours from death. This was beyond my comprehension. What could have possibly gone so wrong at sixteen in this hick town that would warrant a suicide attempt?

He pointed to his wrist and looking at me he asked, "It's pretty obvious why I'm here, but how come you're here?"

Until now, Damian hadn't spoken unless someone had asked him a question. I tried to explain what the doctor and Dave told me about my illness and how I wound up in the padded room.

"It's called bipolar, and oh yeah it's called manic depression too."

Damian looked puzzled, "That's what they say I have."

"Yeah, I read the brochure they gave me and it says mania is one cycle and depression is the other."

We both paused for a moment as we contemplated how we could possibly have the same disorder.

Sara did her part to lighten the mood, "Okay, what's the craziest thing you've ever done?"

"Hmmmm, let me think. That's a hard one," Damian looked down at his wrists.

The contagious laughter spread. Even Kate joined in. Sara made a honking sound as she laughed.

Kate sat back and listened to the three of us trade stories until the nurse came in to close the TV room. That night we all shared a relaxed feeling that none of us had felt for some time.

As we made our way out of the room, Sara pulled me aside, "If you want to come say goodnight, I'll be up."

"Really, what about Kate?" She caught me off-guard.

"Are you kidding, with her pills, she'll be asleep in two minutes. Besides, I want a goodnight kiss from someone I actually like." She walked away and smiled back at me.

I thought to myself, "This is incredible. I'm in a mental ward and I can still hook up with girls!"

Damian had seen how Sara and I acted with each other all day and he overheard what she said.

"Have fun, she's nice. I need to go to bed," he said as he left the TV room.

"It's not like that," I smiled.

"Whatever, man. I'm depressed, not blind," he grinned.

The fact that Damian had a sense of humor made me feel even better. I sat on the main couch and pretended to read magazines to make sure Kate had enough time to fall asleep. When the nurse on duty went to make a phone call, I ducked down the hallway in stealth mode to Sara and Kate's room. I opened the door and listened. Kate snored like a bear.

"You made it," she said lifting the bed cover. I whispered, "Listen, I think you are an amazing person and I know you must think all guys are jerks…" She gave me a peck on the lips to shut me up.

Sara laid down the ground rules. "I know you're a good guy. I'd be bored out of my skull if you weren't here. And so you know, I'm not having sex with you. I just want to kiss you."

"Okay, I just don't want things to get weird," I said seriously.

"Weird? Look where we are, it's way past weird," she said.

After a few seconds we kissed passionately, bodies pressed against each other, hands everywhere. She put her hand on my chest, kissed me on the neck and giggled, "I must have a thing for crazy guys."

Just then we heard someone in the hall.

"You better go." Sara kissed me one last time.

"I crawled slowly out of her bed, making as little noise as possible.

"Be careful sweetie," she said as I looked around the corner.

"What are they gonna do, kick us out?"

"Good point," Sara whispered.

The nurse on duty turned into the first room on the wing. I ran back to the bed and kissed Sara on the cheek then ran to my room and dove onto my bed. The nurse came in seconds later preceded by a flashlight beam bouncing around the room.

"What's that noise?" the nurse asked.

"Oh, I just had to go to the bathroom." I said a little out of breath.

She shined the light around the room and then shut the door.

"Close call," a voice came from the dark.

I forgot about Damian.

"If you're still wondering why I'm here, it's because of a girl." Then he turned over.

It took me a second to figure out what he meant.

"A girl? Are you crazy?" I whispered loudly.

"I'll tell you about it when I'm not so tired," he mumbled.

He's so young; he probably didn't even have his driver's license yet. Damian was out cold before I could press for details.

The excitement of sneaking in Sara's room and kissing her triggered the tempered yet ever-present manic side of my brain. I closed my eyes but couldn't sleep. My watch read 11:30p.m. I wondered if my ex-girlfriend Tara was at a party or if she had a new boyfriend. I missed her more then ever and I fantasized about Tara visiting me on Wing 7. I grabbed the Walkman out of my bag and tried to find the tape she gave me. When I couldn't find it I settled for James Taylor's *Greatest Hits*. Listening to the words I came up with an idea guaranteed to make her fall madly back in love with me. I went into the bathroom and put a towel across the doorjamb so no light would show through the crack.

I had a small voice recorder for class lectures. My idea boiled down to singing the words from James Taylor's *Greatest Hits* and work Tara's name into the songs. A James Taylor Mad Lib of sorts. Over and over, I listened to each song so I could get it just right. On a pad of paper I wrote down the lyrics. All the words seemed to fit the situation so perfectly. "Suzanne, the plans they made put an end to you" became "Tara, the plans we made put an end to me." I re-wound and fast-forwarded until I got all the words down, then I would sing my version into the tape recorder as I listened to it on the Walkman.

This bathroom recording session went on all night. My singing voice amazed me. I believed these recordings could easily be picked up by a major music label, but money wasn't my motivation. I genuinely felt these songs were the way to Tara's heart. I came out with versions of *Fire and Tara*, *Tara on my Mind* and, of course, *Sweet Baby Tara*. I couldn't wait to see her face when she listened to the cassette.

Morning rolled around, another wonderful day began on Wing 7. I wanted somebody, anybody, to wake up so I could play my future Grammy-award-winning songs. Kate had been up since 4:00 a.m. and couldn't get back to sleep. She was the first one lucky enough to hear my late-night musical masterpiece.

"Pete, that's creative," she said graciously. It might have been better, if she'd slapped my face and tried to shock me into reality.

When I wasn't playing my tape to whoever might walk by, I spent the majority of the day trying to focus on the spring break company that I wanted to operate. The fact that I lived in a mental ward and didn't have a nickel to scratch never crossed my mind as a potential obstacle. I took the advertisement out of my bag and dreamed of being paid to sit on a Mexican beach with tanned bodies surrounding me. *Fantastic Visions* was the perfect name for my company. I would start with vacation tours and branch out from there. Even though I started to like Wing 7, I still needed to get back to campus as soon as possible to get the business started.

After breakfast, I went to the magazine rack to look for a logo, something that screamed, *Fantastic Visions!* I worked feverishly, going from magazines to newspapers to magazines, and I began to draw the attention of everyone on the wing. The nurses were looking over and making sure I wasn't bothering anyone. Esmerelda would walk up every couple of minutes and ask if she could help. I would try to show her how to rip pictures out of the magazines, but she would laugh and walk away. Then it dawned on me. I would be the logo! I had some pictures in my knapsack of prom. One showed me getting out of a limo in a tux and looked presidential. I thought this would be the perfect image for my business cards. What better representation of this great company than its founder and president? I located some high school pictures in my bag which helped me make a collage that I would use as the main marketing piece. I mixed the photos with magazine cut-outs like a soaring bald eagle, an American flag, and a classic gold pocket watch. I had no idea what these images had to do with student vacations, but I liked them.

As I feverishly dug through every magazine and book available, Dave came over and asked if I wanted to toss the football.

His voice broke me out of my frenzied state. "Come on Pete you need some fresh air." I followed him down the hall.

The metal door in the exercise room led outside. Additional floors of the hospital partially surrounded this roof-area, making it possible for people to look down at us. Patients were allowed access to the roof a couple times a day with a nurse or orderly present. Damian, a nurse, and two other patients were by the door smoking cigarettes.

"Go long." Dave cocked back his arm.

I caught the ball and did an end-zone style dance.

"Damian, get out here and we can run some plays," I bellowed from the other side of the roof.

"Thanks, I'll pass," he said, holding up his wrist and smiling.

"Shit, I totally forgot," I apologized.

Still smiling, he gave me the middle finger.

While Dave and I passed the ball I watched a nurse who looked like she was kissing the wall. A puff of smoke appeared. She turned around with a lit cigarette. They'd built a contraption to light cigarettes because lighters and matches were forbidden on Wing 7.

Dave got a page on his beeper then went inside. I sat next to Damian and asked if I could bum a cigarette.

He looked at me and laughed, "You want a smoke?"

"Yeah, why wouldn't I?"

He smirked and said, "Sorry, I just figured you for a jock, with the haircut and the football and all."

"Jock? Are we in the fifties now? And who are you, the Fonz? Give me a damn cigarette."

"You never saw a jock smoke?" I said as he watched me fumble around with the wall lighter. I sat down, but he just shook his head. I babbled away as usual. When I stood up to go inside, I had an intense head rush.

Damian looked at me and said, "You're a strange dude." I took it as a compliment.

That night, Damian, Kate, Sara and I watched TV again. We had frequent interruptions from Esmerelda that were more entertaining than anything on TV. She would stand under the TV trying to act out what played on the screen. I'd stopped asking questions when it came to Esmerelda. Eventually, the ladies called it a night. Sara kissed me on the cheek and whispered, "Come see me later."

CHAPTER NINE

Day Twenty Six: Damian's Story

September 26, 1989

Damian asked me if I knew how to play chess.

"Chess, of course I can play chess." I hadn't played in years.

We went to the side of the room where all the games were stored and I grabbed the chessboard. We pulled out our pieces and I watched the day nurses exchange places with night shift as Damian set up the board. Damian began to ask me questions about the game; I knew I was in trouble.

Damian made the first move by bringing a pawn out two spaces.

"What kind of tapes do you listen to?" I asked.

"Have you ever heard of Nirvana? They kick ass," Damian said with more excitement then I thought he had in him. As he told me how his friend made a bootleg tape at a show in Seattle, his face lit up and for a few seconds I saw the real Damian.

As we talked, the rules of chess slowly came back to me and I began to plot out my moves. While we played, Damian's scars showed each time he made a move.

"So tell me about the girl," I asked.

"Girl?" Damian replied like he didn't know what I meant.

"Yeah. You said the other night you'd tell me when you weren't so tired."

"Oh yeah, about my…" he looked down at his arm. "I'm staying away from girls forever," he said without looking back up.

"Staying away from girls? Are you high?" I said.

"I don't know what happened exactly. I meant Heather, my ex-girlfriend." He emphasized ex. "But now I don't know what to think, I'm still trying to figure this shit out," he said with frustration.

"Man, no girl is worth that."

"It's hard to explain; I've been trying to figure this shit out the last couple days. I know she's a part of it, but it's more than Heather," Damian said, frustrated.

"I'm sorry. I didn't mean to say it like that," I retracted.

He leaned halfway over the chessboard so no one else could hear him. "I can't remember when I've ever felt normal."

Damian spoke with such emotion that I thought tears were coming any second. I am glad I had the presence of mind to shut up for a minute and listen.

"When I see people normal and happy, it pisses me off so bad. After the first time I cut myself I had go to a shrink. He sucked. I hated him. The medication made me sick, so I stopped taking it. I had no energy, I mean nothing. Listening to music in my room and seeing Heather were the only things I could stand. Everyday I'd wake up to my alarm, start to get dressed for school, and then crawl back to bed. I felt like I weighed a thousand pounds. My mom and dad were freaking out, but I couldn't do anything about it." Damian paused.

"Heather constantly threatened to break up with me but she would always come back the next day. I don't know why she didn't end it sooner, I was in bed sometimes for days at a time. I mean who the hell wants to be around someone who hates everyone and everything and sleeps all the time." Damian said, grinding his teeth.

"You know, I think the drugs they have me on this time are working, because at least I can talk about it. Right?" he asked with intensity.

"Yeah, that's true," I said.

He rubbed his hands over his face and through his hair.

"I just want to get the fuck out of this mess so bad. I'll do whatever they say this time. I don't want to die."

He looked at the board. "It's your turn."

Distracted by his story I moved my queen into a vulnerable position. Damian took a deep breath and continued.

"Anyway, the week before Heather left for a three week trip to her Grandma's house our arguments got much worse. The night before she left we got into a massive argument and she broke up with me for good. I can still hear Heather screaming at me, 'You're a fucking loser!' I tried to call her the next morning, but she never answered. She left without talking to me."

"That blows." I said.

"I've never been so angry, I planned to steal a car and drive there. A few days later, she calls from Florida, and I thought for sure she would miss me, the same as I missed her. She said, 'Damian, I don't love you anymore.' It rang in my ears over and over. I couldn't get the words out of my head. I pleaded, then begged her to change her mind. She hung up. I kept calling until I got her back on the phone. By the time she picked up I'd almost destroyed my room," he gripped the table as he spoke.

"Listen, my parents are gonna call the police if you keep calling," she said as if she didn't even know me. Then she hung up for the last time. Nothing made sense. I imagined Heather would magically come back on the line and make everything okay. She never did.

"Soon I wasn't thinking about Heather anymore, my thoughts went beyond the relationship. Every part of my body and mind felt like a black-hole sucking the energy from everything around me. I sat in my chair, shivering from fear. Everything had become so shitty and I had no idea how to get back to reality. I didn't notice that the glass in my hand shattered. I swear to God, I never said to myself, 'I think I'll slice my wrist to pieces tonight.' I actually felt nothing. I promise I didn't do it on purpose." Damian looked at me to see if I believed him. I gave him a reassuring look and he continued.

He lowered his voice. "I didn't just pick up the piece of glass and start cutting. The whole thing was like an overpowering itch.

"It sounds stupid, but when I scratched the shit out of my arm with the broken glass it felt good. The fucking itch wouldn't go away and scratching was my only relief. I couldn't stop. But the scratching wasn't necessarily connected to the horrible thoughts that played over and over in my head. I couldn't escape. Rubbing the glass on my arm seemed totally separate. I can't explain what the hell I'm talking about." Tears streamed down his face.

He used his sleeve to wipe his eyes and said, "The last thing I remember was a warm sensation on my arm and thinking, what the fuck did I do? I must have done a pretty good job this time. I cut real deep. My parents came home from the movies and found me on the floor with blood still pouring out of my arm and my room demolished. They thought I'd been attacked. The doctor told me that if my parents hadn't found me when they did I'd be dead."

Damian looked in my eyes. "But Pete, I swear, I just want to be fucking normal again."

His emotionally packed story had me stunned. I didn't know what to say. He seemed relieved to be able to get it out in the open. I was honored that he opened up to me.

"I'm sorry, I must look like I'm the biggest pussy," he said pulling up his shirt to wipe away any remaining signs of tears.

"Heather's the only other person I've ever told any of this shit to."

"You can talk to me anytime you need to talk, I'm your man."

We didn't have to say anything else, we knew we were both confused.

I looked down at the checkered board. "Let's finish the game."

"I'm gonna kick your college ass!" Damian had regained his composure.

While we made our last moves I remembered that Damian said he had bipolar disorder, the same as me. In some ways I looked at Damian's bandage with a touch of jealousy. His scars provided visual proof of his illness to the outside world. So far I only had the doctor's explanation to go on. I compared the energy that kept me awake for weeks running around with that stupid puppet to Damian's inescapable itch. I wondered if the black-hole that pushed Damian to slash his wrist the same, only in reverse? This marked the first time I was able to compare mania with depression.

My king was toast in three moves. A nurse came out from behind the Plexiglas. We were the last ones up. Even Marathon Man had disappeared.

"Come on Bobbie Fischer, time for bed," she said with a heavy New York accent.

As I said goodnight to the nurse, a yawn interrupted my sentence. For the first time since the padded room, I actually felt tired.

"Are you tired?" Damian asked, seeming surprised.

"I guess I am," I shrugged.

I tried to play it off like nothing, but a huge smile came across my face. We put the game away and headed to bed. I forgot all about going to Sara's room.

"Hey man, I don't know exactly what is going on in your head, but it's not worth dying for," I said, staring up at the ceiling from my pillow.

"I know, don't worry. I'm taking the meds this time," Damian said in the darkness.

With that, my eyes closed.

CHAPTER TEN

Day Twenty Seven: The Fog Begins to Clear

September 27, 1989

The next day I woke up stretching with a sensation like the first warm day after winter, when you can tell that spring is coming. I opened my eyes, I couldn't believe the clock read noon. I'd slept through breakfast. I guess the nurses wanted to see how long I would actually sleep. I threw on my jeans and an army t-shirt. Kate, Damian, and Sara were all hanging out in the main room, smiling at me.

"Sleep well?" Sara asked.

"Yeah. I guess I did, huh?" I shrugged, acting cool. I wasn't back to normal, but a definite change had occurred. Sara and Kate said that I talked slower and that my eyes were not darting back and forth as much as when I first arrived. Noticeably, I was able to concentrate for longer periods of time and have somewhat fluid conversations.

The way Dave, Sara, Damian and Kate treated me, it could have been my birthday. I loved the attention. Breakfast had come and gone, but Sara saved me a box of Coco-Pebbles and a carton of milk. I went into the TV room and she sat down close to me. I felt her hand on my knee. I guessed she forgave me for not stopping by her room last night.

"You missed all the commotion last night. Marathon Man swallowed an entire bottle of Johnson & Johnson's shampoo, or at least I think that's what they said," Sara told me.

"Yeah, they took him to the emergency room early this morning," Damian chimed in somberly.

"Is he all right?" I asked.

"He'll survive, but Kate said he threw up at four in the morning. I could smell it when I got up," Sara said. Kate nodded in agreement.

"Wow, that sucks."

"I heard the nurses talking, and they said they're gonna transfer him to the state hospital for good," Sara finished.

"I'm gonna miss him," I said looking down the empty hallway.

The rest of the day I continued to work on "Fantastic Visions" and studied the subjects I needed to catch up on for school.

I had the ability to concentrate long enough to read chapters in a book.

That night I went outside with Damian and Sara to have a smoke. Damian went to use the bathroom, and the nurse went to take a phone call, leaving Sara and I alone. We stood next to each other, and she gently grabbed my hand. I was still charged with sexual energy. She looked at me as if to say, "I don't mind." Once we realized no one was around, our hormones got the best of us and we were all over each other again.

"Do you want to do something crazy?" I asked her.

"Of course," she said.

"OK, hear me out. When you go back in, go take a shower like normal. I'll pretend like I'm going to take a shower. If it's clear, I'll sneak in with you."

She looked up in the air then answered, "I told you we can't have sex."

"I promise we won't go all the way, but we can still have fun," I said, putting my hand up her shirt like we were in eighth grade and kissed her.

"OK, let's do it." She whispered with a smile. "Give me ten minutes." She kissed me once more then hurried back inside. I was so excited!

Sara went to her room and I went into the TV room to tell Damian not to wait up for me. He shook his head and kept flipping through the stations. At 8:00 p.m. the wing already quieted down. Two nurses on duty talked to each other and were not paying any attention. I was home free.

After a few minutes, I grabbed my shower stuff and a towel and jumped into one of the open shower rooms. I got undressed faster then a stage actor. I walked out into the hall with just a towel and made sure no one saw me. One door had the red occupied sign showing, I turned the handle.

"Is that you?" Sara said nervously.

"Yeah it's me," I whispered.

The steam from the shower filled the room, but I could see movement behind the curtain. I opened it slowly and there she stood. She looked beautiful. Her hair pulled back and wet, her body looked better then it felt.

"Wow, you're amazing."

"Turn the light off, I'm shy," she pulled the curtain so it covered her.

"You shy? Who are you kidding?"

But I wanted to play by her rules. So I hit the lights, dropped my towel and got in. I couldn't believe my luck. I dodged the hot water until I got used to it. We bumped against the walls of the tiny shower, trying to find a comfortable spot. The stream from the showerhead was powerful. Kissing and getting sprayed in the face wasn't the same as it looks on TV.

I spun around to move out of the jet of water when all of a sudden I slipped with Sara wrapped in my arms. Bam! My whole body smacked into the hard plastic of the bottom of the shower. It sounded like a bomb went off. We held our breath and lay there naked in darkness with water pouring over us. My head had hit the edge of the tub and it hurt like a bitch.

"Are you all right?" we heard as the door handle opened and the light switch went on.

"Yeah, I'm fine, I just slipped," Sara said, putting her hand on my mouth.

"Why was the light off?" the nurse said, opening the shower curtain without warning. "What is going on? Get out!" the nurse said to me with disgust.

I slipped as we both tried to get up. I made it to my towel, and then scrambled back to my clothes in the other shower room. I got fully dressed, afraid to come out and face my punishment. I felt horrible for Sara, trapped and getting lectured by the nurse. I finally stepped out to face the music.

The nurse pulled me by my arm and brought me to the main room.

"Listen, son, do you know where you are?"

"Yeah," I replied with a guilty look.

"What are you thinking? Well, obviously you're not." Her nametag said Margaret Kelly RN. She reminded me of the lady who scheduled detentions back in high school. If it meant a trip to the padded room, it would have been worth it.

"I'm sorry. We didn't mean anything,"

"Listen, do you know what would have happened if that girl wanted to get you in trouble? Just be glad she told me the truth." The anger in her voice had changed to pity.

"If you want to get out of this place, you have to behave. Do you understand me?" she said.

"Yes. I'm sorry. It's all my fault," I said.

"I'm not going to write this up, but the nurses are going to watch both of you closely from now on. If anything like this happens again, you'll be extending your stay here. I guarantee it."

That was the last thing I wanted. Sara's a wonderful girl, but I wanted to get back to college more than anything. We were going to have to be careful from now on.

"Get back to your room and go to sleep," she said sternly.

Breakfast the next morning was awkward. Damian looked at Sara, then at me and shook his head. Sara just kicked me under the table. Kate had no idea about the shower incident.

Kate's husband Neil came to visit with Jacob. When Neil put the baby in her arms I could see her pride.

"Is this the guy you were telling me about?" Neil asked.

Kate nodded.

"My wife says you've been an inspiration to her. Thanks for that," he said, shaking my hand.

"Cool. I didn't know I'm an inspiration, but Kate's doing a lot better then when I first met her."

"Seems like you both are from what she tells me. Nice to meet you," he said as they moved over to the couches.

The rest of the day we hung out on the roof, smoked cigarettes and watched stupid television. I spent some of the day reading college textbooks. The nurses organized a board game group that night and everyone voted on monopoly. A few of us played with the nurses, and the rest were half-hearted spectators. The game got competitive. Damian and the nurse battled it out for Park Avenue. In the end, Damian walked away with most of the monopoly money.

I missed exercise class the next morning because Dr. Verrett came to evaluate me. He had a nurse come by to draw my blood.

"Pete, from now on you'll have to check your blood about every three months to make sure that the medicine is at the right level in your bloodstream." he explained in a serious tone.

The nurse pulled up my sleeve and wrapped a piece of rubber around my arm. She smacked my arm a couple of times and I laughed out of nervousness. The needle stuck in, and blood spurted into a small tube. I figured if this is what I needed to do to get out of here, I was all for it.

"I should have the results back in a couple of days, then we can tell if the levels are correct for you. We may need to adjust the dosage and evaluate you for a short while longer. So far, you're doing great, and if you keep it up, you'll be out of here sooner than you think."

"A few days just to get results back? What are you talking about? I thought I would be out of here in a few days! When will I get out of here?"

"I can't say Pete, we just have to make sure your level is right. There's no definite time frame--it's up to your body. It depends on many things. Just keep doing what you're doing. But I advise you to take cold showers from now on. Alone, that is," the doctor said without smiling.

"You heard about that," I said with a guilty look.

"I hear everything. Remember, if you want to get out of here sooner than later, the first thing to do is to play by the rules. We're observing you to see how the medication is doing, not to baby-sit. I'll leave it at that."

The doctor looked at me as if he knew my thoughts, and I could tell he felt bad that he couldn't give me a straight answer.

"It won't be days, but it won't be long if everything goes as well as it has," he said, trying to empathize.

"I don't understand. I'm fine! What are you looking for?" I asked in frustration.

"Please, Pete. I can't say what I'm looking for--it just has to happen. We're dealing with powerful medication. If we don't have the time to get the levels right, it can be dangerous. We'll do our best to make sure you have everything you need to stay on track here. You need to trust me."

It had been less then a week since I'd walked out of the padded room, but it seemed like forever. I was livid. Looking away from the doctor, I gazed out the window and felt like I'd break down if I opened my mouth. I bit my tongue, thinking to myself, God I hate this feeling. It fucking sucks. It took me a minute before I could speak. I took a deep breath.

"Well, can I at least get a pass?" I said, narrowly holding back the tears.

He pulled his chair close.

"As soon as the tests come back you'll get a pass. In the meantime, some of your friends from Bloomsburg have already arranged to come by. I normally don't let patients have visitors this soon, but I'm making an exception," he smiled.

"Friends? Who's coming?" I was thrilled to have visitors.

"Well, I spoke to a young lady by the name of Krissy, and she asked if she could bring some friends over. I told her visitors are only allowed for a half-hour at this time."

"Krissy's is coming? That's great! When?"

Doc Verrett looked at his watch, "Today. I'm pretty sure she said about lunch time."

I focused on getting ready for my visitors. I wondered who was coming besides Krissy. It felt like the President of The United States was on his way. After taking a long shower, I rubbed gel over my head to spike any of the hairs that were sprouting up.

Before I knew it, I heard a commotion at the main doors. I turned back to read my books and make it look as if I hadn't been waiting for them. Krissy walked in followed by my friend from basic training, John Kelly, and his father. An even bigger surprise was seeing Steve, my friend with the puppet, Jerry, the Kirk Cameron look-alike, Slater and Clorinda file in. My mom held the rear of the line, smiling from ear to ear. I couldn't believe they all came. Josi was the last in line, and she wouldn't let me out of her hug.

"Please, you're embarrassing me," I said.

"Oh, my boy is back!" She hugged me again.

"You look great," Krissy said.

"I look great for being in a mental ward, I guess."

Krissy rubbed the stubbles on my head and John punched me in the arm.

"This is nice. Better then Fort Knox, that's for sure," I could tell John felt awkward, but that soon disappeared. I gave my friends the grand tour of Wing 7. I asked Esmerelda to tell them about her hamster. She acted shy for the first time. The guys from the dorm loved her and seemed to like the place. They were cracking jokes within a minute or two. I showed them the roof, and no one could believe we were allowed to have cigarettes in a hospital.

"How cool is that," Steve said about the lighter on the wall.

Jerry flirted with a nurse. "I'm in pre-med, maybe we can study together sometime." She just smiled and ignored him. Doc Verrett gave the okay for my visitors to stay twenty minutes longer, so we all played catch. For a second, I felt like one of the guys again. Finally, time was up.

"Get back soon. That girl Sherry asked about you," Slater confided.

"Get me her phone number," Jerry whispered, pointing to the nurse.

Krissy hugged me goodbye.

"You get better and come see us in Wilkes-Barre, OK?" Mr. Kelly said.

"You get your ass squared away Private. You hear me boy?" John said in his best drill sergeant imitation.

"I'm gonna visit as much as I can," Krissy promised as they all walked out the door.

They will never know what that visit meant to me.

As the days in the hospital passed, I continued to show signs of slowing down. My mom had camped out at a hotel next to the hospital and she visited everyday. I was glad to see her but, like any teenage male, I got annoyed hanging out with my mom after a few minutes.

My blood test came back from the lab.

"Just be patient with me and you'll have the life back you had. That's all I can say," the doctor said after explaining the positive results.

He still didn't give me any time frame.

A couple of days later Dave came in and told me that my mom and dad were coming to talk with the doctor and they wanted me to join them.

"My dad? What the hell is he coming for?" I asked.

"I don't know, why?" Dave said.

"I haven't talked to him in a year. I don't want to see him."

"Well, he's coming. Just get through it, okay?"

"All right, but I'm not taking any shit from him,"

Josi came in first. I could tell she'd been crying again. "The Captain," my dad, came in a few minutes later and deliberately stood about ten feet away from my mom. My father was a retired fighter pilot in the Navy. He also had a serious problem with alcohol. My brother , sister and I called on Father's Day and Christmas, but that's about it. My parents had separated for the second and final time three years ago but it should have happened years earlier. To the outside world my father seemed a great guy--neatly dressed, handsome. But the real Jim Barnes could be a viscous and sometimes violent person when fueled by alcohol. The problem for us was that he drank almost everyday I had known him. I've always known deep down that he has a lot of problems that I did not understand, but that didn't help me hide my disgust in his presence.

Doc Verrett had finished saying hello to them one at a time and now they all walked down the hallway. Josi had a plastic bag with her. It held toothpaste, cards, and a BLT sandwich.

"Are you hungry? Can we get you something from the cafeteria?" she whispered as if they were starving me.

"No, I'm fine. I already ate," I said, trying to get her to stop.

The two of them were making me feel like they were visiting me in jail. We all sat down, and for a minute or two the mood bordered on pleasant. In no time, the conversation erupted into a blame game between my mom and dad. Nothing had changed. Here we were in a mental ward, and they were practically screaming at each other. The behavior was absurd and sad.

Josi continued to ask questions about medication and my treatment. I'd made great strides from the week before, and Josi was thrilled for me. My father, on the other hand, tried to figure out who was to blame. Josi had no luck trying to explain what had happened. He insisted that the term "mental illness" was a complete sham. He didn't hide his belief that the doctors, the university, and my mom were all quacks.

"See, I knew something like this would happen if they grew up with you and your crazy relatives," said "The Captain," raising his voice, but at the same time gritting his teeth to try and subdue the volume.

"What about you and your family? They're way more screwed up than our family could ever be," was Josi's retort.

My dad turned to the doctor for reassurance, "You can see how she ruined our marriage, and now she's messed up our son, too."

This went on and on. Each tried to count crazy people on each other's family trees. The truth is that both families had a lot of branches to pull from. I guessed that Doc Verrett wanted to punch my father almost as much as I did. He acted extremely diplomatic, given the language tossed around.

My father had traveled three hours for a chance to put down my mom, who was in jeopardy of losing her job because she'd decided to stay close to the hospital. Finally, I broke in. "You know what, you haven't changed, you're still an asshole, just get out, no one wants you here anyway!" I said, standing in front of him. The noise we were creating set off the signal for all nurses and orderlies on deck, to come to the scene.

There had been many times in my life when my father and mother blew up at each other in public. Let's see: Little League games, first dates, and even at high school graduation. Why should this be any different? I was upset because he embarrassed me, in what had become my temporary home.

"Don't worry, you little mamma's boy freak. I am leaving, and I'm sorry that crazy family turned you rotten." He spit as he spoke.

I followed him as he stormed out.

"If anyone in this family is crazy, it's you!" I belted down the hallway as I watched him get on the elevator. He always called my brother and me "mamma's boys" when things didn't go his way. If bipolar was genetic, then I probably inherited it from my dad's side. He made me more determined to stick with my treatment. Maybe if he had gotten some help he wouldn't be so screwed up.

I asked my mom to wait upstairs until my dad left.

"Don't worry about me, you just keep getting better," Josi said.

I wanted to make sure that Dave and a couple of security guards went with her, when she left. She could always handle my dad so I wasn't too concerned, but I worried that he would be waiting downstairs to give her hell in the parking lot. Back in the main room, Sara and Damian were waiting for me. Sara came up to me, gave me a hug, and rubbed my back. We went out on the roof and Damian and I smoked a cigarette.

"Man, I thought my parents were bad," Damian said.

I smiled, "Nothing changes." The subject was dropped.

The next day after breakfast, I got a call. A nurse I'd never met came up to me asking, "Are you Peter? Your brother Paul is on the phone."

I smiled, "Paul? That's awesome!"

Finally I could talk to someone who could understand the brilliance of my ideas. I picked up the phone used by patients to receive calls.

"So dude, what's up?" Paul asked.

I hadn't spoken to him since I'd called him from my dorm room to explain how the world had changed for me.

"You have to hear my idea for a business. I have this company and it's going to be huge," I said.

I was excited to tell him everything, positive he'd have nothing but praise for my entrepreneurial spirit. His response wasn't exactly the glowing reverence I hoped for. A moment of dead silence followed. Then he ripped into me.

"Listen, you better knock off this crap. You're gonna give Mom a heart attack. You know this is bullshit. Just knock it off so you can get out of that place and get back to school."

I found myself defending Wing 7. "This place isn't bad. I'll be out of here in no time. The people are great. They're regulating my medicine because I'm too brilliant for normal society to handle, that's all. When I get out of here, I'll be able to control my brilliance.

Do you realize that Winston Churchill and Abraham Lincoln had the same thing I do?"

On one of his previous visits the Doc had left me with a pamphlet that listed all the famous writers, musicians, actors and great leaders who were bipolar. This list had become a mini bible of sorts to me.

He paused for a second then said, "Yeah, and they're both dead." I could hear utter frustration in his tone. "Just get the hell back to the old Pete." He hung up. I felt like shit after that call, but, I reasoned with myself, maybe he'll never understand my brilliance.

The day filled with contact from the outside world.

"A friend called while you were on the phone. I told her to come over. Krissy's her name, and she'll be here in about a half-hour," one of the nurses told me.

Krissy's coming! I got my things together so I could show her my plans for the company, and I brought my tape recorder so she could listen to my tapes. The nurse also said the doctor had given me a pass to go to the cafeteria downstairs. Fantastic news! I thought. It meant that we could go downstairs and get fresh air on the deck. Dave came up to give me a lecture about the rules. I was allowed downstairs, but if anything happened out of the ordinary, I would not get another pass. He said he would give us space but he had to be downstairs watching us. I looked at him, "Thanks, man. I promise nothing will happen."

Over the loudspeaker I heard my name being called and I rushed over to the nurses' station. Krissy walked towards me looking uneasy. We hugged and said hello, then took the elevator down with Dave. He walked us to the patio of the main hospital cafeteria.

We sat on a ledge surrounded by hedges that blocked the view of the parking lot. The fresh-cut grass behind the hedge gave off a magnificent aroma. Krissy chain-smoked as I began to ramble on about everything that had happened to me since she had last visited. She sat patiently and listened as I played my entire collection of James Taylor rip-offs. I even did some live versions for her. She deserved a medal of honor in open-mindedness for sitting there without laughing out loud. I stopped talking briefly when she told me about her best friends, Becca and Betsy, who lived a few blocks from my brother at West Virginia University. She told me how they were all pulling for me to get out of here soon. Then the time allotted for my pass expired.

As she left, I made jokes and tried to get her to smile. Instead I almost brought her to tears. She hugged me tight and just said, "Get better." This confused me every time someone said "get better." Why weren't they telling me how lucky I was to be so incredibly bright? Like before, I continued to accept their reactions as ignorance and let it go.

After Krissy left, I went on the roof to bum a smoke from Damian. I saw him sitting up against the wall with his head in his knees. I went and sat down next to him. "Do you want to play some chess?"

He looked up at me, wiping tears from his eyes. "No, I don't want to play any fucking chess game."

I didn't understand. An hour ago he seemed fine. He stood up and lit his smoke. I could see his hands shook badly. I didn't know what to say, so I told him about my visit with Krissy.

"Man, don't you ever shut up?" he cut me off abruptly.

I didn't take offense because I knew I was a freaking motor-mouth these days. Now Damian talked fast, slowed only by the deep breaths he needed to take.

"I can't handle anything. I still feel like shit all the time. I don't think my medicine is working and I'm scared. I don't know what I'm gonna do when they send me home. I don't have any friends. You had all those people visit. Nobody wants to visit me. Except for you and Sara, I hate everyone. You're going to leave, and then I'm screwed. I can't remember a time when I was happy." Then he put his head down in between his knees.

"Hey, man, listen, you're gonna be fine, I promise."

I had no idea what else to say. I sat there uncomfortably for what seemed like forever. He wasn't exactly crying now, but his chest heaved. The ember of his cigarette came close to burning his hand. It reminded me of when I sat on the steps of the army barracks and the cigarette burned the tip of my finger. Only instead of feeling that fantastic energy I'd felt, Damian's energy took him in the other direction. We were two screwed up kids, trying desperately to figure out how our minds broke. If the drugs didn't fix us, then what?

Sara came out to see what we were up to.

"Damian's having a rough day." Damian had his head in his knees and rocked back and forth. Sara instinctively sat next to him and put her arm around him. After another ten minutes, he wiped his eyes, said he had to go to the bathroom and went inside. Sara whispered for me to follow. She grabbed my arm as I went back in. "But don't make it look like you're checking on him."

I went back to my room and told Damian through the bathroom door, "Let me know when you're done." He didn't say anything, but I heard the toilet flush and the faucet running.

Damian walked out drying his face with a towel, acting as if nothing had ever happened. I went in and used the toilet. By the time I emerged he wasn't upset anymore. Watching the drastic shift in someone else's emotions was incredible.

The next day came another surprise. Sara was leaving Wing 7. She got the word that her best friend's parents were legally able to take custody of her. She didn't have all the details, but Lori and her parents were picking her up in an hour.

I was sad to see her go, but it's what we all wanted. She packed her belongings, which were nothing more than would fill a small gym bag. Damian, Kate, Sara, and I talked while she waited.

I tried to joke, "What am I going to do without my partner in crime?"

"Well, you have Damian," Sara laughed.

I pulled her close, "But he doesn't kiss as well as you."

She punched me playfully in the arm. "Get out."

Sara excused herself to the bathroom and I became aware of how envious I was of her leaving. Despite that feeling, I was happy that she had people who cared about her.

Not a second after she turned the corner, Sara's friend Lori and her parents walked through the doors and went to the nurses' station. They looked around and seemed intimidated by the surroundings.

"Are you here for Sara?" I asked politely.

They looked at me but past me like I didn't exist. I felt like a homeless guy asking for change.

Sara came back around the corner and when Lori saw her, she ran and hugged her. They came back and Sara introduced me as the guy who had taken care of her.

I went on and on about how Sara would be better off with them. They never said anything to me, they just smiled, probably hoping I wouldn't grab one of them and hold them hostage, or worse. Sara pulled me aside one more time and said, "Listen, Pete, don't let them take anything away from you here. Your ideas are amazing and you're gonna be great." She said she would call me even though contact with patients violated a major rule. "I'll say I'm Tara," she winked.

She kissed me on the cheek then walked out with her new family.

Doc Verrett also came to see Sara off. After she left, he came to talk to me. We sat on the couch as he went over my medication results.

"Your levels are perfect, but I can't let you go yet."

"What is that supposed to mean? I feel great."

He backpedaled, "What I mean is that you are still not completely well, Pete, but you're getting there. The good news is I'm giving you a two-hour, off-grounds pass to go to lunch with your mom and Krissy tomorrow. This is a privilege we don't give to everyone."

Would this bullshit ever end? "Doc, when am I getting out of this place? What are you looking for? I'll do whatever you want. I've done everything you've said."

He looked in the air, trying to think of how to phrase what he wanted to say. "Pete, you're a smart kid. You have everything going for you. It's simply a matter of time. I can't tell you what to do. Does that make sense?"

I picked up a magazine and turned away, repulsed. "It makes about as much sense as everything else around here."

This wasn't the news I wanted. The human terrarium was starting to piss me off. I finally saw this place as it was, a place for people to sit and wait while the people behind the glass looked at us and made little notes based on whatever they felt like. The doctors would make celebrity appearances every few days. In a lot of ways, Wing 7 was like any other floor in the hospital. But instead of being laid up in a bed, we were confined to this wing waiting for medication to do its magic. I was sick of waiting.

The next day, Krissy and Josi showed up around 10:00 a.m. Dave gave me a refresher of the rules. As we walked across the parking lot, I pressed Josi to see if she knew when I'd be released. She didn't seem to know any more than I did.

We ended up at the Pine Barn Inn Restaurant, the only place within walking distance of the hospital. After we sat down to eat, I told my mom the great plans for "Fantastic Visions." She had less patience than Krissy. As I explained my ideas, she began to cry. I'd never seen my mother cry like this.

"Do you realize if you keep this up, they're going to keep you here for a long time? I can't take it anymore. You have to stop all this!"

The waiter looked over and Krissy tried to calm her down. Fear came over me, like I did something terribly wrong, but I didn't know what. I grabbed Josi's hand "I'm sorry, I promise I'll get out of here soon." She somehow pulled it together by the time the waiter came back, and we all ordered our meals. She managed to shut me up for a minute to tell me that the lady from the university would be meeting us at the hospital soon.

"Mrs. Masterson is on her way to meet with us this afternoon to talk about going back to Bloomsburg. Please don't talk about this company nonsense," she said.

What incredible news! We didn't say much more, and I enjoyed my first taste of real food in some time. The fresh salad and clam chowder were amazing.

After the meal, the three of us walked back to the hospital. The sun shone and a refreshing breeze made for a perfect combination. Josi decided to read a book and wait for Mrs. Masterson. Krissy and I hung out in a courtyard near the main entrance. Right on time, a nurse came to escort me back to the wing.

I was amped at the possibility of getting back to Bloomsburg. I found Damian on the roof and told him how much fun he would have if he came to visit me.

"You can come when you get better. I promise you'll forget all about Heather as soon as you see all the college women." He rolled his eyes.

"I told you I'm staying away from girls."

"Yeah, but these are women."

"Whatever."

"Pete Barnes to the front desk," came over the loudspeaker. Damian walked to the nurses station because he had a question about his medication. Doc Verrett, Mrs. Masterson, and Josi all waited by the nurses' station. This time I wanted to kiss her phony ass so she'd let me back in school. I said hello and she gave me a smile and nodded her head.

We went into the TV room. Esmerelda stood in the doorway; the doctor escorted her out and turned off the TV. Mrs. Masterson glanced around the room uneasily. She leaned over and told Doc Verrett that she had a meeting on campus directly after this one. She did everything but check her watch to let us know she did not want to be in this room and the feeling was mutual.

Doc Verrett started the meeting awkwardly with a summary of my progress. Josi sat next to me, and Mrs. Masterson directly across the table. Mrs. Masterson wore a business suit that made her look serious. It featured a variety of brown colors woven into a plaid skirt and a brown and beige sweater. She had nice legs, and if she ever smiled, she might even be considered an attractive woman.

However, her ice-cold personality created an ugly layer that made it almost impossible to see any of these attractive features.

The doctor, taking a seat next to Mrs. Masterson, acted as a mediator. It didn't take her long to get to the point. She smiled as she said, "Well, Peter, we are so glad you're doing better. However, you won't be able to attend Bloomsburg University this fall."

She was matter-of-fact, like an insurance claims person on the phone telling you, "I'm sorry, your accident won't be covered. Have a nice day!"

The words were devastating to me. I'd played their game and now they were turning their backs on me. As I spoke, I tried not to show my feelings. I didn't want to give Mrs. Masterson the satisfaction. "But you said if the doctor gave the OK, I could come back. That was the deal."

"You have simply missed too many classes to be let back in this semester. Quite frankly, it wouldn't be fair to the other students, now would it?" she stated in a robotic tone.

In shock, I looked around the room to see if anyone else shared my horror.

Then Josi spoke up, "But you told me if he kept up his studies and recovered here that he would be allowed back into school."

"No, Mrs. Barnes, that is not what I said," she replied as she started to fold up her notebook. "At this point, they will not allow Peter back in the dorms. He threatened a dorm manager, not to mention me. That alone is worthy of expulsion. Quite frankly, he's lucky none of this will be recorded on his transcript. Pete is considered a risk. The good news is that we have arranged for Pete to get a full refund on your student loans."

"Threatened? I never threatened anyone, what are you talking about." I said standing up.

Peter sit down let me talk." Josi said forcefully. I sat down.

"Then your saying if my son lived off campus he would be allowed back in classes?" Josi asked.

"I am sorry, it's not going to be possible. Well, I must get to my next appointment," Mrs. Masterson said standing up.

Josi looked furious, but tried to keep her cool. "He's no harm to you or anyone there. He's doing great. He's been studying and probably knows more than half the kids. He's finished all the work your advisor sent."

"You promised. I remember you said if the doctor gave the okay, I'd be allowed back," I repeated.

"Only because you wouldn't agree to get help. We said that for your own good." she answered abruptly.

She was about to ruin all my plans! My emotions boiled to anger. I tried to hold my tongue but I could not. "You are a liar, what kind of university would hire you in the first place." I said with a dramatic flair. "I may be crazy but you're a cold rude person and you don't know two shits about psychology or me." I tried hard not to curse and I came close but she pissed me the hell off. I slammed the door behind me but it was one of those doors that has an air piston to make it close softly, which only frustrated me more. I was devastated.

I paced the hallway in the same way Marathon Man had. The three of them stayed in the room, and I could hear a heated discussion between Josi and Mrs. Masterson.

With each minute, my rage grew. The doctor came out and grabbed my arm. "Pete, listen, we know you're upset but this is not helping. If you ever want me to release you, you can't act like a child."

I looked at him with revulsion, "You all lied to me! What the hell does it matter what I act like? I'm in a mental hospital with a bunch of people lying to me. I could act like a monkey and it wouldn't make any difference." I didn't trust anyone at this point.

"Peter, I don't know what they told you to get you in here. I wasn't there. You must understand I've never lied to you and I never will. If you ever want to get back into any university, I need you to sit here and calm down." He pointed me to a couch. "This lady might be rude, but she can screw up your future if you aren't careful."

As soon as I sat down, Damian came over to see what happened. I spoke, choking out every other word, almost as much as he had on the roof the other day. I tried to explain. He looked in the direction of the TV room, "Ah, that's bullshit."

Then the doc came and motioned for me to come in.

He did most of the talking this time. "Pete, you've made great progress, and you will be out of here in no time if things keep going well. You won't be able to go back to Bloomsburg this fall. It's simply too far along in the semester. However, Mrs. Masterson has agreed to allow me to submit a letter of recommendation that will help when you are considered for the spring semester starting in January."

Mrs. Masterson looked at me. "I understand you're frustrated, but that's all we can offer right now."

The doc looked at me and said, "Now please apologize for your earlier comments."

"I'm sorry for cursing, it's just that I've been studying hard." I felt like a five-year-old.

She smiled back, saying nothing, gathered her things and proceeded to leave the building. The doctor commended me for my apology, and Josi seemed to be in a better mood. She stayed and talked to the doctor for a while. I wanted to hide. I went back to my room and laid on the bed.

212

CHAPTER ELEVEN

Day Thirty Two: Can I Leave Now?

October 2, 1989

My strategy shifted dramatically that day. Up to that point, I might as well have been dressed up in a cheerleader's outfit with pom-poms trying to please the doctors and nurses. My focus changed from running a company to getting the hell out of this place. Until that day, my desire to get out was linked to the pursuit of my ideas. Now I just wanted to see my friends and get back to life as I knew it before this manic episode ever happened. Even the food started to drive me crazy. I focused all my energy on getting out.

That night, Damian and I played chess again and talked all night long about what we were going to do when we got out of Wing 7. He was glad to have someone to talk to who wasn't so damn happy all the time.

A few days went by, and I didn't once talk about Fantastic Visions. My conversations with the Doc changed, too. Instead of trying to convince him how great I felt, I just answered his questions directly.

My speech pattern and physical behavior continued to slow. Most noticeably, I consistently slept through the night.

The nurses had given us the freedom to go on the roof without them coming out with us every time. We spent most of our free time smoking out there. The temperature dropped every day, but right now the sun felt warm on my face. A child looking down from a few floors above waved to us. We waved back, then Damian gave him the finger. The gesture was returned, and the onlooker disappeared.

We decided to go back inside and watch TV. As we walked in, we heard a loud shriek coming from the direction of the elevators. Then we heard sneakers screeching across the linoleum tile, bodies shuffling and a hail of curse words flying. The screams got louder and louder as the doors swung open. In the middle of the pile a pale little girl emerged, no more than fifteen years old. She looked over at us, laughing hysterically. She wore handcuffs that were giant hoops around her tiny wrists. For a moment, she relaxed and one of the nurses undid the handcuffs. When the handcuffs came off the emaciated girl lifted up her t-shirt, showing us her bare breasts. Her ribs were almost poking through her skin.

"Is that what you wanted to see, you fags? I am an electric super goddess!" she said, wildly laughing at us. She sounded like the girl in the exorcist before her head spun around.

A female nurse quickly pulled her shirt down.

Now we could only see her head poking out of a web of arms. Looking at us with eyes that might pop out of her head, a hoarse voice yelled, "You guys wanna double team me? Come over here, I'll bang both of your brains out! Come on, you know you want to fuck me, fuck me, fuck me, fuck me!" she said this while pretending to have an orgasm right there. She jumped up and down like a child having a temper tantrum, saying, "What's the matter, are you guys gay? Aren't you man enough? Come over here. What's the matter? Are you scared?"

We were speechless.

Then she let out a freakish, shrill laugh. She sang, spelling out the word fuck, "I am gonna fuck you guys, F-U-C-K, you both. I am gonna fuck all of you freaks!"

The gaggle of nurses, security guards, and orderlies finally rushed from the nurses' station into the back hallway.

Kate came up behind us. We all looked at each other.

"Holy shit, what the hell was that?" Damian said.

Kate turned to him and said, "You should have seen how Pete looked when they dragged him in punching and kicking."

My heart sank, and I didn't know what to say. She was right. The eyes—how she spoke--I looked like that before they put me in the padded room. I understood now why my friends and family had seemed frightened of me. "I hope she doesn't have to stay in the padded room long," I said.

In the afternoon, Krissy made an unexpected visit. "I had to get away from classes. They're so boring."

"So you came here for excitement. You're sicker than I am."

I got a chance to introduce her to Damian. They hung out and smoked a cigarette while I went to the bathroom.

Damian came back with a smile on his face for the first time in days. "Hey man, she's nice."

I looked at him and laughed, "I thought you weren't going after women anymore."

"Well, yeah, but she's nice, and did you see that red hair?" he said.

"I don't know if sixteen-year-olds are her thing, but I'll see what I can do."

He grabbed my arm. "No, don't say anything, please."

"Don't worry, I won't screw it up for ya, I promise." For a second we both sounded like normal teenagers.

Krissy and I took a walk on a path around the front of the building. I didn't bring my music or my notes about the company down with me this time. A nurse watched me from the porch on the cafeteria. I told Krissy what Damian said and she turned bright red.

"Great, maybe after you leave, I'll come back and pick up some guys," she said sarcastically.

"Hey, he's actually a great guy." I said with earnest.

"Actually speaking of guys, that is one of the reasons I stopped by, I have kind of been hanging out with John," she blushed.

I stopped walking and looked at her. "John? I knew it. He asked me about you."

"We kinda went out on a date last night," Krissy said.

"Yeah and…?"

"We went to a party. He walked me home. Pete he's a complete gentleman." She smiled.

"So that's why I got the surprise visit," I laughed. "John's a lucky guy if he gets to date you."

"You think he's a good guy?" Krissy asked, looking for a stamp of approval.

"Are you kidding? John's a great guy. This could be the best thing that's happened from all this crazy shit."

We sat on the ledge of the garden and she put her head on my shoulder.

Hey Krissy, can I tell you something?" I asked.

"Sure," she said.

"They brought this young girl in and she's manic. It freaked me out to see how I was. I'm sorry if I scared you."

"You have nothing to be sorry about. You're doing great. I am so proud of you," she said, looking up at me.

"I'm not proud, I feel like I just woke up from a nightmare. I'm so embarrassed."

"Pete, believe me, you shouldn't be embarrassed at all. People have already forgotten about the things you did."

"Yeah, I guess you're right."

"The guys from the dorm keep asking about you. I think you're lucky to have so many people looking out for you. By the way that guy that looks like Kirk Cameron told me to remind you that he wants the nurse's phone number," Krissy said, lighting up another cigarette.

She made me feel good. Never once did Krissy talk down to me. In high school, we were just casual friends. Now she visited me in a mental facility on a regular basis. In situations like this, you hoped your family would look out for you, but you couldn't expect it from mere acquaintances. The way she treated me helped me feel like my old self.

Krissy had tears in her eyes. "Don't worry, I'm not upset."

"So why are you crying?" I asked puzzled.

She hugged me harder than anyone had in a long time.

"You're doing so well. Keep it up, you hear me?" she said, walking away.

"Tell John I said he's a lucky guy!" I yelled down the hall.

When I came back to the wing, I found Damian on the couch. He acted cool like he didn't care if I'd talked to Krissy about him. "Man, she wants you bad."

He looked up with wide eyes. I couldn't screw with his head. "No, I'm joking. She's already dating someone, but she said you were really nice."

He looked back down at the *Better Homes and Garden* magazine he pretended to read.

I looked over his shoulder and said, "Nice magazine, getting some good tips?" Then I jumped on the opposite couch. "Don't worry, she has a lot of friends."

That night the usual suspects minus Sara watched TV. Our otherwise pleasant night occasionally interrupted by faint but chilling screams coming from the direction of the padded room. Kate and

Damian felt wiped out by their medication and went to bed by nine. I stayed up to watch an old rerun of *SCTV*. Martin Short played Ed Grimley.

The TV show had lulled me into a semi-hypnotic state, when suddenly fingernails were gouging my throat. Before I could turn around, the grip tightened. Had the new girl somehow broken out of the padded room? I managed to turn my head to see Jack, red faced with veins popping out of his head. For an old man he had fierce grip, and within seconds I couldn't breathe.

He must be on his drug dealer kick again, I thought. I grabbed his arms in an attempt to break his grip. When that failed, I used my body weight and flipped him over the couch. Never releasing his grip until in mid-air, he landed squarely on the coffee table then bounced onto the floor. He must have been close to a hundred pounds. Like a zombie that wouldn't die, he tried to get up and come after me.

"What the hell is wrong with you? For the last time, I'm not a drug dealer!" I said, as he grabbed my ankle.

"You and your goddamn drugs killed my boy," he said from the floor, hyperventilating. I thought he might have a heart attack right there.

"You never had a boy," I screamed at him.

A nurse and a security guard grabbed Jack off the floor and rushed him out of the room. "Fucking murderer! Piece of shit drug dealer! You deserve to die!" Jack yelled at me from down the hallway.

As I caught my breath, the orderly held my wrist firmly to ensure I wouldn't go after him.

"I swear I didn't start anything. He came from behind me and started choking me! Look," I said, pointing to my neck. I had deep scratches where Jack's long fingernails had dug in.

The commotion had stirred almost everyone out of their rooms.

"What the hell happened?" Damian asked.

"That crazy old man," I said, still out of breath.

"Leave it to you to get strangled by Grandpa," Damian walked back to our room.

Just another day on Wing 7, I thought, looking at my neck as I brushed my teeth. That night, many thoughts raced through my head. The girl from earlier, Jack, Krissy, my brother--all came in and out of my head. I realized, at this time of night most of my college friends were probably getting ready to go out for the night. I pictured John and Krissy eating pizza at Sal's and my brother and our friends partying at WVU. I'd never been so jealous of other people in my life. Up until now, I'd felt superior. Lying in this lonely hospital bed was the last place I'd ever imagined I'd be at this point in my life. Envy was all I could feel.

I woke up early and I went to the bathroom and washed my face. In the fuzzy mirror I noticed that I looked better, healthier. I took a hot shower and got ready for the day. I looked out the window, for a moment being inside wasn't bad. The wind blew sheets of rain sideways and lightning flashed.

After Dave signed in about 9 a.m., he came and apologized for what happened with Jack. Dave didn't blame me. He told me that Jack had been put into a padded room while they adjusted his meds.

After breakfast, I felt an overpowering need to get out of this place. I got on the phone and called Josi at the hotel. "Listen, I'm better now, I swear. I promise I'm ready to come home, I can't stand it in here anymore!" She tried to explain what the doctor told her about my medication.

"Please, just get me out of here!" I begged.

I went to the room we used for exercise and started to do push-ups. I needed to get any extra energy out. I didn't want to give them any reason to keep me longer.

Dave walked in, "Are you all right?"

"I'm cool. Just working out," I said, still doing push-ups.

He could hear my frustration. I felt trapped.

"Pete, go wait on the couch and relax for a minute, I'll be back."

I grudgingly complied.

He left, and I envisioned all of them coming back and putting me in the padded room. I wanted to run and make a break for it.

Doc Verrett came through the nurses' door. He had a strange look on his face. He sat down and put his arm on my shoulder.

"Listen, Pete, you're getting out tomorrow," a huge smile took over his face.

I looked at him like a five-year-old, a second or two later the words sunk in.

"I knew that would shut you up. I've been checking your lithium levels and everything seems to be going great. You've been observed and your behavior is consistent with the medication levels. It will take some time for your body to get used to the lithium, but it's no longer necessary to keep you in this hospital. We were going to wait to tell you tomorrow, but Dave felt it would be better if you knew today,"

The only thing I wanted in the world had just come true. It could not have been better timing, because while I did my push-ups, I'd plotted my escape.

I grabbed the Doc's hand and started to shake it. "I promise you're not making a mistake." To make sure he wasn't playing any head games, I asked one last time, "No tricks? I'm getting out?" He nodded his head.

I went up to Esmerelda and hugged her as hard as I could. Next I found Kate. In the past few days, she'd retired her old robe and began to wear normal clothes. She even pulled her hair back with a scrunchy. Kate congratulated me. I ran into my room to tell Damian. I had to wake him.

"Good for you," he said in a dull, sleepy voice, then he went back to sleep.

Damian's mood seemed to get worse, not better. He slept a good chunk of time. My promises of college women and fun times to come didn't work. When awake, he kept trying to call someone on the phone. I am sure Heather is the one he called. She never answered.

CHAPTER TWELVE

Day Thirty Eight: Leaving "Wing 7"

October 8, 1989

The rest of that day and night were the longest of my life. The next morning I woke Damian up to say goodbye.

"If you get out of here and get your head on straight, I guarantee Krissy will introduce you to her friends," I said.

"Listen Pete, thanks," he said rubbing his eyes and trying to wake up.

"For what?" I asked.

"For being the first college kid I've met who wasn't an asshole," he smiled.

"Promise me you won't ever pull that crazy shit again?"

"Don't worry, I'm cool. Now get out of here before they change their minds."

"Look me up when I get back to Bloomsburg next semester," I said, walking out the door of our room.

All the orderlies and nurses came to say goodbye and wish me luck. The doc and Dave were waiting for me.

"Do you think he's ready for the real world, or should we keep him for a few more days?" Doc Verrett joked to Dave, then got down to the business at hand.

"I set up a meeting with Dr. Miller back in your hometown. He sounds like a great doctor and he knows what he's talking about. Here's a three-month supply of the medication you need to take every day, twice a day." He handed me a bottle. "Dr. Miller will be the one to prescribe your medication from now on. You'll need to keep up with the blood tests and follow simple rules and otherwise live just like you did before. Just stay healthy. No offense, but we don't ever want to see you here again. Your mom said she'd meet you downstairs at eleven o'clock," Doc Verrett finished.

Dave spoke up, "I've seen too many people come through this door and their medication never takes--be glad yours did." Then he gave me a football guy's type hug where you give a quick slap on the back.

Kate walked up to me and gave me a hug, too. "Pete, I'm so glad you were here. You don't know how much it meant to me to have so much energy around."

"You take care of Jacob," I said with a lump in my throat. Saying goodbye to my friends on Wing 7 was difficult.

CHAPTER THIRTEEN

Day Thirty Nine: Pancakes and a Dose of Reality

October 9, 1989

When my eyes opened and I wiped the drool from the long ride back from the hospital to Valley Forge from my chin, I realized we were back in our neighborhood. The cars in our parking lot were the same. It looked almost as if the world had stood still.

I felt exhausted. After I brought my bags into the house, I told Josi that I wanted to get some sleep. Josi wouldn't argue with that. We'd arrived in the middle of the afternoon and everyone I knew worked or at went to school. I went straight to the basement, threw my stuff in the corner and crashed hard.

I didn't wake up until the following morning. I awoke to the mouth-watering smell of bacon and pancakes. I could hear feet walking above me, and I went upstairs. Harry and Diane were sitting at the table while Josi buzzed around the small kitchen. They both welcomed me with hugs. Josi announced that the pancakes were ready. This was the first breakfast in memory where I didn't grab coffee and a piece of fruit and run out the door. Refreshed and eager to talk with my sister and Harry, I poured a cup of Josi's java and sat down. The coffee tasted as terrible as I'd remembered. My silverware and plate were already out in front of me. Next to the plate were my pills laid out like vitamins. I swallowed them down.

"So what do you want to do for your birthday, old man? It's coming up pretty soon," Diane asked.

Dates hadn't crossed my mind in a while, let alone my birthday.

I looked at them, puzzled, "What day is it?"

My mom and sister began arguing over the date. Harry pointed to the ninth of October to end the discussion.

"Same old, same old?" he said shaking his head.

I wanted to be normal in the worst way and now I was. I ate everything on my plate and began to tell stories about the characters in the hospital. We laughed as Harry related his version of my escape from the house. Then Josi broke in with her version of stories about the hospital. We interrupted each other as we tried to describe Esmerelda. An hour flew by before Harry and Diane had to get to work.

As they left I got a call from my brother, happy not to be talking to me in a mental ward.

"Everyone's asked about you at Becca's party last night," Paul said. He paused for a second. "Hey, I know things are screwed-up for you right now, and I'm sorry if I was an asshole before. I was worried."

"It's cool, I know."

"Come down here as soon as you can, and we'll celebrate our birthday. We're almost nineteen years old. Can you believe that? I talked to Todd and Brian and they said they wanted to road trip down here. You should all come. We'll have a blast," he said.

He put our friend Chris on the phone.

"Your brother is the biggest sap. He met this girl for like two seconds and he's in love. Anyway, come on down so we can bust his balls. Take care of yourself and say hi to Josi for me," Chris finished.

"I will. Tell everyone I said hi," I said before I hung up.

I pictured them all sitting around on beanbag furniture and bunk beds with a beer in one hand and the phone in the other. I worried that everyone would walk on eggshells around me and they weren't. I don't know if they did it consciously, or if it just came naturally, but I'd never appreciated the sounds of their voices more.

My second day back and Wing 7 faded into a memory. Things couldn't have been going smoother.

230

CHAPTER FOURTEEN

Day Forty Three: Round Two

October 13, 1989

While I was at the hospital, my brother had arranged a job at Shramek's, a local gas station where he'd worked during high school. The station was run by Jake and Drew Shramek, they'd taken over the business about ten years ago, when their father "Big John" Shramek died of emphysema. Paul had worked there junior and senior year in high school. The station, a short walk from the house, offered me an opportunity make some cash while I reapplied to Bloomsburg. It also made for a good excuse to get out of the house. Paul told the owners about my time in the hospital, but they didn't bring it up when I met with them about the job.

I started working in the morning. Something seemed different. I couldn't concentrate. Fleeting thoughts of a more efficient full service and brilliant marketing ideas floated in and out of my head as I pumped gas. I saw new ways to make the gas station better everywhere I turned. I wanted it to become the best gas station in the history of gas stations. I even had a sudden renewed interest in Fantastic Visions. While these grand plans took over, I lost my ability to concentrate on the most basic of tasks. Making change for customers became a monumental event. I couldn't add or subtract-- nothing came easily. I ran back and forth, cars lined up. I kept making mistakes.

Despite my shortcomings, I still felt the need to tell the owners how to make the business better. I wasn't making any sense to them. The morning of my third day, they pulled me aside. Drew blamed a $200 discrepancy in the register on me.

"Listen Pete, we know you have been through a lot, but this just isn't working out," Jake said with Drew next to him.

Devastated and embarrassed, I couldn't respond. These guys weren't the type of guys you could cry in front of, but unexplainably I was about to burst out in tears. Jake understood that I wasn't the same Pete that visited his brother at the station for years. Drew on the other hand, had always been a jerk and hadn't changed.

I heard them talking in the office. "I knew hiring a fucking whack-job was a mistake. He probably stole it," Drew slapped a tire iron in his hand as he spoke about me. I scrambled to apologize.

"I never would take a dime. Besides I have ideas that will make you millions if you have a minute." I pleaded.

"Listen I did your brother a favor, just get your crazy ass out of here and we'll call it even." Drew said, going back under the hood of a car.

"You know how Drew is, don't pay him no mind. But I'm afraid we can't have you working here. Here's the money we owe you and don't worry about the register, we'll figure out where it went." Jake said handing me two hundred and forty dollars in cash.

I left the garage mortified. What would Josi say? Pissed at Drew for being such an asshole and at myself for losing a gas pumping job, I ran back to the house. By the time I reached the front door, the idea for "Fantastic Visions" had retaken its position as my top priority. I wanted to get back to the basement so I could complete the work I'd started in the hospital. I slammed the door behind me and made a beeline for the stairs.

All the material from the hospital still sat in my bag unpacked. I pulled out the "Fantastic Visions" collage I created on Wing 7, it screamed at me, "I AM YOUR SALVATION!!!" This echoed in my head as I struggled to make sense of my behavior. Unlike before, I knew something wasn't right and I tried to fight against it. But the urge to create a business overpowered me. Again, my perceived brilliance of these ideas began to outweigh any doubts.

Without the limitations of the hospital, I could now bring my project to life. I spread out all the material on the floor. I brought down the portable phone and began calling every vacation company I could find in the phone book. By the afternoon, I'd called over fifty travel agents and any other travel-related businesses that happened to be in the book. My efforts had landed me over a dozen appointments. This success sent me into a frenzy.

This time I wouldn't tell anyone my ideas until the money rolled in the door. I'd surprise everyone. Nothing could stop an idea like this, not doctors, not nurses. All the obstacles had been removed.

I needed more supplies for my collage, which would serve as a marketing display at my meetings. I planned on taking the two hundred and forty dollars as my seed money to make billions. I took it and made my way to find a copy machine. I walked and ran, walked, ran, till I made it to our local supermarket. My emotions changed fast. When I reached the store, I went right for the photocopier. Lori, a friend from high school tapped me on the shoulder.

"Pete, you're back. How come you're not up at Bloomsburg?" she said in her bubbly cheerleader tone.

She got more than she bargained for. I tried to tell her everything that had happened over the last few months. I kept talking, ignoring the signals she gave indicating she wanted to leave. Finally, I stopped for a breath of air.

"Pete, it's great to see you, but my boyfriend's waiting in the car," she said, walking away abruptly.

"Great to see you Lori!" I sounded a bit desperate.

I tried to make copies but the machine took my money without printing the copies. I banged on the machine to try and get a refund. I found myself in tears trying to explain what happened to the store security guard. He asked me to leave the store.

I didn't want any trouble so I walked back home. "Why is this happening to me? I'm supposed to be better. I'm not supposed to be fucking crying," I said to myself out loud. I thought maybe the medication caused my shift in emotions.

Josi took time off from work to bring me a sandwich at the gas station. When she found out I'd been fired, she raced home in a panic.

In the basement I continued to get ready for my appointments. I would need to look sharp. I went upstairs to put on a suit and tie.

I heard Josi as she walked in the front door.

"Peter, are you home?" I heard from my bedroom.

She went directly down the basement stairs and almost had a heart attack when she saw the magazines cutouts everywhere, pages ripped out of the phonebook, and the Fantastic Visions collage.

I ran down to ask her how I looked in my suit. Instead of being excited about my imminent success, she started to cry.

"What are you doing? Please no, please!" She went from crying to screaming. Pick up all this shit off the floor! They said you were going to be fine! I can't believe this!" Then she picked up the portable phone and ran up the stairs.

Since we had been through this routine before, I did not overreact. She would understand once the business started bringing in money. I continued to try every combination of clothing in my closet. Each time I came down to get her opinion, she yelled something to the effect of, "Stop it. Please stop it. I can't take this anymore."

"No one in our family will ever have to work again," I yelled from the top of the stairs.

Josi didn't know what to do. My sister and Harry had both gone to Colorado to visit Harry's cousins. While I tried on the clothes, she called Dr. Miller and got his answering machine. After leaving several messages with friends and family asking for help, my cousin Brandt called back first.

Brandt is my closest cousin; we've hung out since we were in diapers. After my mom told him the story, he grabbed some clothes and drove in from his dorm at Temple University. While he drove to my house, the doctor called my mom and said to get me to the hospital immediately.

I refused to go. Brandt patiently hung out in the basement with me the entire night. He and my mother tried to persuade me to go for help until late in the night.

"Aunt Josi, I'll watch him until morning. We'll try again in the morning; I'll make sure he doesn't go anywhere. Go get some sleep," Brandt said.

Josi went upstairs but she never slept.

I continued to explain my business ideas to Brandt. I didn't take off my suit because I wanted to head out on appointments first thing in the morning.

But instead, Josi and Brandt took another stab at convincing me to go to the hospital. Josi had been on the phone with

Dr. Miller, and he arranged for me to be accepted into Paoli Hospital's psychiatric unit to determine what had gone wrong with the medication.

"Mrs. Barnes, this isn't uncommon. Let's just figure a way to get him safely to the hospital. Can you put him on the phone?" Dr. Miller asked.

He asked me how I felt and again I spoke of my exciting business plans. I liked this guy. He promised that my mom would give me the car to go on the appointments if I took a simple blood test.

"Yeah, I might be able to do that," I said.

I handed the phone back to Josi, "Do whatever it takes to get him to the hospital. I'll take it from there," he said.

Sensing my mom's fear, I agreed to go take the blood test at the hospital. Before I knew it, I unknowingly signed papers again, allowing my admittance to the hospital's mental facility.

Another episode was underway, different from the first, this time triggered by an adverse reaction to Tegretol, one of the prescribed medications. It disrupted my concentration and I could not hold back my emotions.

I spent my nineteenth birthday in a padded room similar to the one I stayed in the first few nights at Geisinger. My actions and energy level virtually identical to the first padded room. After a few days in the hospital the Tegretol was out of my system. It took the doctors one week to make the adjustments and another for them to observe me. When the correct levels were reached I felt like I'd stepped out of a dense fog and into a clear blue sky.

CHAPTER FIFTEEN

Day Sixty

October 30, 1989

I truly felt like the old me. I wasn't scared or confused anymore. I only wanted to get back to life. I made plans again, but this time they did not include becoming a world famous D.J., a puppeteer or a mogul in the student travel business. This time I simply wanted to go back to school and be a normal college student. I would do whatever it took to get there.

CHAPTER SIXTEEN

What's Up, Doc?

November 3, 1989

Following my release from Paoli Hospital, I returned home. I adjusted to the grueling schedule of being out of school and out of work. I now knew far more than I would like to admit about daytime soap operas. Josi made sure I squeezed in a meeting with Dr. Miller. I wanted to show him the real me. Most importantly, besides Doc Verrett, he held the power to advise the college on my health status.

I'd been out of the hospital almost a week, but Josi was still reluctant to hand over the keys to the car.

"You know I'm fine. I only want the car to go to the doctor's and right back. Please, I need you to trust me if I'm going to get back to life," I whined. After a mini lecture of everything she had been through over the past few weeks she handed me the keys.

It took me a minute to get the feel of the gears again, but driving gave me a sense of normalcy. I cranked up the radio and made my way across town. I found the office and even had a few minutes to spare. I pulled into the parking lot of an old, Victorian-style duplex that had been converted into offices. For a brief moment, I felt anxious and an urge to turn around swept over me.

Nevertheless, I continued up the stairs and opened the door. A lady wearing bi-focals greeted me with a warm smile. When I told her that I had an appointment with Dr. Miller, she handed me a clipboard with a lot of questions: name, address, billing information and about fifty questions about my health history.

"Fill out those papers and give them back to me when you're done, please," she said in a pleasant receptionist tone. I filled it out the best I could and handed it to her.

"That's fine. Now go through the door marked Dr. Miller and he will be with you shortly," she said and pointed to a door.

The waiting room was the size of a hall closet with a separate exit and had the stale smell of mothballs.

I had visions of lying on a couch and being analyzed and probed with all sorts of questions about my past. I heard muffled voices behind the door, but I couldn't make anything out. Finally the door opened. A woman emerged; she didn't look me in the eyes and quickly went out the door. Then Dr. Miller turned to me, shook my hand and introduced himself. I remembered him from the earlier hospital visit but like all of my memories of mania it felt like recalling another person's memory. His handshake felt fragile and warm.

Dr. Miller was a skinny man; his hair lay flat on his forehead. He wore a pale yellow shirt, a solid brown tie with a fat knot and a tweed coat-jacket with brown patches on the elbows. The solid wood desk filled the majority of the room. Behind the desk stood a tall bookcase with hardback medical journals stacked to the top. Small wooden African statues adorned the desk, along with a picture of his family. They looked like a serious group, in contrast to the "Far Side" daily calendar next to the picture. He pointed me to a chair in front of his desk.

I was antsy, but not nervous.

"So how does this work?" I asked.

"How does what work?" he looked at me, puzzled.

"These meetings," I replied.

"Do you remember me?" he asked.

I scratched my head, trying to figure out how to answer.

"I met you, but I wasn't the same."

I tried to explain. He let me talk until silence filled the room, never interrupting me. Most of what I wanted to know revolved around getting back to Bloomsburg.

"Why do you want to go back?" he asked.

"Well, first of all, I need to get out of my mom's house. Secondly, I want to get a degree," I said matter-of-factly.

Like Dr. Verrett, he stroked my ego by listing all of the great leaders, actors and creative people who shared the same disorder. This time I could soak in what he said. Next he began to explain in simple terms why I could never drink alcohol again.

"It's simple. When lithium enters the bloodstream, it alters sodium transport in the nerves and muscles, creating a sort of magical balance. If the levels go up or down, you have a chance of becoming unbalanced, hence the name 'chemical imbalance.' If you drink alcohol, it dilutes your medicine, therefore making it useless. You could have a beer today and you would be fine, but over time it would change your levels. Drinking dramatically increases your chances of cycling back into a manic state. Even cough syrups and other products that have alcohol can alter the levels if used regularly. Does that make sense to you?"

I smiled and looked him in the eye and said, "I've already accepted that. I'll do whatever it takes not to go back to the hospital. Besides, I'm not a good drunk anyway, or at least that's what my friends tell me." I was being honest.

"Peter, this is not a joke. As a matter of fact, I can tell you that eighty percent of the people who walk through my door with that smile wind up back in the hospital. The best and worst part about bipolar disorder is if the medicine works you feel perfectly fine, and some people decide they no longer need to take the medicine.

I cannot stress this enough, Pete. Staying away from drinking is one of the only things that you can control. I can't make any of my patients do anything. This is the only time I will ever have this conversation with you. I don't like wasting time," he said calmly but forcefully.

Doc Verrett had told me about the affects of alcohol, but not with this much conviction.

He made sense.

I'd read about all the possible side effects from Lithobid in the brochure. He went over them with me and told me that weight gain, liver problems and shakiness of the hands were possible side effects.

Then bing, a timer went off. It had been forty-five minutes, but it seemed like we had just started.

"Well, Pete, I can tell you're doing a great deal better than our first meeting. Let's keep it that way," he said, standing up and shaking my hand. I thought of a hundred other questions, but he walked me to the door and said, "See you next week at the same time."

Now that wasn't so bad, I thought getting into the car. I didn't feel any pressure. I looked forward to the next meeting.

CHAPTER SEVENTEEN

Welcome Back "Francis"

November 3, 1989

That night a good friend from high school called my house. Josi handed me the phone, Todd the biggest smart ass of all our friends, said, "So I hear you got out of the loony-bin. We're picking you up to celebrate."

"Cool, when are you coming?" I said, laughing.

"Why, do you have something better? Just be ready, dingleberry." He hung up.

The fact that he made fun of me was a great sign. I'd been afraid of how my friends would react to me. I dreaded trying to explain what had happened.

My closest friends Brian, Scott and Todd picked me up and we started driving to Casey's, a local bar. I sat silent in the back seat. "What's the matter, Francis, you can't talk?" Todd said, and they laughed. Francis was a crazy character from the movie *Stripes* that we had all watched together before my brother and I left for basic training. I love them for having the balls to call a guy that just walked out of a mental ward "Francis." It made me feel good to know they weren't going to treat me any different than they did before I went into the hospital.

As we walked into the bar, I explained why I couldn't drink. Brian patted me on the back, "Good, then you're driving home!" He bought me cokes all night to help me avoid awkward conversation about why I wasn't drinking. Scott caught me up on how the Eagles were doing so far this season. Nothing had changed.

Todd had invited his friend Susan. It turned out he invited her because her brother had bipolar, and he thought we would have something to talk about. He was right. Susan and I talked the entire night. She had a lot of questions; I felt like I helped.

The truth of the matter was that it didn't bother me that I couldn't drink. In comparison, drinking water in a bar with my friends beat the alternative. If I could only cut down on the cigarette habit I'd developed I'd be home free.

I ended up crashing on my buddy Brian's couch. He complained about living at home. "How am I ever going to get laid living with my mom upstairs?" Then before he went up to his room

246

he said, "Hey man, it's good to see you're back to your old self. I don't know if you remember calling me from the hospital, but you scared the shit out of me. It's great to have the old Pete back. You know we're all here for you man, no matter what. Plus, now I'm not the only loser living at home."

"Yeah, don't remind me," I said, putting my hands behind my head.

That first night out with my friends meant more to me then they could ever know. All my fears had been for nothing. I had good friends who actually were proud to be seen with me. That felt unbelievably good.

CHAPTER EIGHTEEN

Back to Bloomsburg

January 17, 1990

Besides wanting to get out of Mom's basement, the reason I never gave up on getting back into Bloomsburg was simple, stubborn pride. This pride included an intense desire to prove Mrs. Masterson wrong. Sometimes anger can be a great motivator. I didn't tell anyone, but my ultimate satisfaction would be the look on her face when I first walked past her on campus.

I knew if I didn't go back there, then I would always have a place in the world that just wasn't right. I desperately wanted to put everything I'd been through behind me. I wanted to face my fears head-on. I thought if I could just get back to Bloomsburg, I would make every day count.

After writing and submitting my application and waiting for weeks, I got a letter in the mail. I opened it, a wave of relief swept over me. Back to Bloomsburg!

It had only been five months but it felt like a lifetime. When I moved back to campus at the beginning of the next semester, I tried to keep a low profile. I wasn't sure how people would react to me. My new room in the same dorm as John Kelly's suited me fine. Dan, my old dorm manager, knocked on the door as I unpacked my belongings.

"Pete, how are you doing?" he said, sitting on my new roommate's bed.

"I'm doing okay. I'm glad to be back,"

"We're glad to have you back; the dorm staff knows what happened to you but they are all in your corner. I've been here ten years and you aren't the first person who's been through this type of situation. Don't be afraid to come to my office anytime." His sincerity made me feel at home.

"Thanks. That's cool of you to say and I'm sorry for..." He cut me off.

"You don't have to be sorry for anything. Just make sure you kick ass in your classes this semester. That's all anyone is going to look at in the end."

"I've had a lot of time to think about what's important to me and getting good grades is the only thing on my mind right now," I said.

"Great. If you put half your energy into studying, my money says you'll get a 4.0 grade average. Remember, my door is open," he said, leaving the room.

I took a walk around campus; I knew I'd be fine. Maybe because my hair had grown back or I'd blown my situation out of proportion, but the feeling of wearing a huge "I'M CRAZY" sign on my back disappeared. Not only did no one notice me, but all the people from my old dorm treated me exactly like my friends from home had. Within days, we were in the cafeteria trying to get phone numbers again. This time, I played it low key, but I still had fun. My biggest fear of being the laughing stock of the campus had been put to rest. Day by day my confidence grew.

Krissy and John had dated for a month but were now officially not dating but still "good friends." John had joined TKE, Harry's fraternity, and they asked me to pledge the following semester when I was eligible. Krissy, John and I got to be even closer over the years. Jerry or "Kirk" ended up marrying the nurse from the hospital. I'm kidding but it did take him almost a year to stop asking for her phone number. Going back to Bloomsburg ended up the best move I could have made.

CHAPTER NINETEEN

No More Itch

April 21, 1990

I'd been back on campus for a few months and spring had begun. I hadn't stayed in touch with anyone from the hospital. In some ways, I'd subconsciously blocked my memories of the hospital the moment I stepped back on campus. I took my medication everyday but I'd almost convinced myself they were ordinary vitamins. I was enjoying a relatively normal college life.

Then one afternoon I walked downtown to grab a slice of pizza from Sal's. In the distance I saw Dave, the orderly from Geisinger Hospital. He walked with a group of friends. I almost hoped he wouldn't recognize me, but he did. Dave's face lit up when he saw me, and he told his friends he would catch up to them. They kept walking toward campus. Dave asked how I'd been. I told him the short version of the last few months. Memories rushed back. I asked about everyone. He'd heard Sara moved to Arizona with her new family and she loved her new high school.

"How's Damian doing?" I asked.

He looked at me as if he didn't know what to say.

"Pete, I thought you knew. The story made the front page of the local paper a while back. I don't know how to say this. Damian's gone; he died," he said, looking at the ground.

My jaw hit the pavement. I didn't know how to react. I pressed for details. Dave told me Damian left the hospital a week after me and he seemed to improve. He somehow hid the way he felt from his parents. Two months later his parents went away for the weekend for the first time in a year. While they were gone he shot himself with a gun he stole from his neighbor.

I wanted to puke. Dave knew how I felt. "I'm really sorry," he said, "some people just don't get better." "Thanks for letting me know," I said. "Pete, you look really good, take care of yourself, OK?" Dave said with sincerity. "Same to you," I replied. He gave me a genuine hug, and then turned to catch up with his friends.

In a daze, I walked past the pizza place and kept going. I felt like such a piece of shit for never getting a hold of Damian. The people in the hospital had been a million miles away until this moment. Now it felt like a huge demolition ball had slammed into me.

Every conversation came back to me. I pictured Damian fighting the itch he had explained. I couldn't get the image of him lying lifeless on the floor out of my head. I turned into an alley because tears were starting to pour down my face brought on by an overwhelming feeling of helplessness. I closed my eyes and pictured Damian sitting on the roof of Wing 7 smoking a cigarette, middle finger in the air, grinning ear to ear. No one close to me had died and I wasn't prepared for this news. I leaned against a dumpster and slid down until I was sitting on a pile of cardboard boxes, then I let it all out.

I was terrified of the fact that we shared the same illness. I thought back to the massive energy I felt sitting on the stairs of the army barracks. I envisioned that energy in reverse. Then everything Damian and I had talked about our illness became clear. That energy I felt that kept me awake for weeks must have been the same exact energy he felt only in reverse. A healthy person would never consider running thirty miles up a turnpike with no water. Just like a healthy person would never take their life. Without a doubt, I saw clear parallels between mania and depression. A healthy person has something stopping them in their brain, a built in defense system. No matter how bad a healthy person feels, they won't kill themselves. Their mind stops them and allows them to think of alternatives and consequences. In the mind of a clinically manic or depressed person that defense system is not functioning, there are no other solutions. It's my belief that this is purely related to chemical reactions in the brain and should be classified as a physical disorder in these cases, not mental. Medication simply didn't work for him the same way it did for me. Lithium gave me the ability to get back to reality and make decisions from a rational point of view. A deep sadness came over me knowing how hard he fought to feel better. Sitting there, head in hands, frozen, I prayed to whoever was out there that I'd never end up in Damian's shoes.

Epilogue

My friendship with Damian and my understanding of how depression relates to mania has scared me enough to stay on what I feel is the right path for me. I want to restate that my diagnosis was Bipolar I. There are different forms of bipolar and the treatment for each are not the same.

In the years following this story, I can honestly say I've led the best life I know how. I have come to look upon my experience with bipolar disorder not as an illness, but rather as a gift of heightened senses. I've stayed true to my pledge of never touching a drop of alcohol. While at Bloomsburg, I did everything I could to make the most of my second chance. I started using my energy productively and focused on reasonable goals. I loved my major, Mass Communications, and eventually did host a radio show--just a normal radio show--as I had to explain to my mom. In my junior year, I was elected vice president of student government in the largest voter turnout in school history. That news made Josi cry in a much different way. During my two-year term as vice president, I had the pleasure of saying hello to Mrs. Masterson every month at the Board of Trustees meetings. I don't need to explain how much I loved that. I also became the first non-drinking social director of the Bloomsburg chapter of the Tau Kappa Epsilon fraternity. Including the manic semester. It took five years, but I eventually graduated with a 3.6 grade-point average in my major. Thanks to good friends like Krissy and John, my college years were as crazy as they should have been. The Army National Guard allowed me to complete my six-year term without any questions. I had no further incidents. I thank the people in charge for having open minds.

The past thirteen years my career has consisted of various advertising/sales positions. Other than taking medication and avoiding alcohol, I have never let this disorder dictate my life. Seven years ago I moved halfway across the country, where I knew only one person, and made a life for myself. I have learned to snowboard and even completed a triathlon. I have a great group of friends who support me.

Despite amazing efforts by books, movies, television programs, and advocacy groups like NAMI (National Alliance for the Mentally Ill) to combat the stigma of mental illness, a deep misunderstanding of mental illness still exists around the world. Many people still believe that mental disorders are caused by negative social conditions or even lack of good parenting. I believe strongly that bipolar disorder is a genetic brain disorder. I am proof. My evidence is my twin brother Paul. Paul and I grew up in virtually identical worlds. We were raised in the same dysfunctional

256

household, attended the same school system, and shared the same friends. We even completed army training together and started college at the same time. All of our major social and economical influences were indistinguishable, yet Paul has never experienced a manic episode. This simple fact is all the proof I need that mania is what the doctors say: a chemical imbalance. Bipolar disorder is no different than an insulin attack or any other physical disorder that requires a patient to take medicine on a regular basis. This has helped me in my internal struggle to understand manic depression.

Every day, like it or not, I'm reminded by four small pills that I'm bipolar. It's a small inconvenience for sanity. I am convinced this medication has saved me from a tormented life. I have suffered no major side effects that I know of from Lithobid. My last manic episode was in 1989. Lithium is a miracle drug as far as I am concerned. But I feel living a healthy lifestyle is equally as important to staying out of the hospital, or worse.

It would be false to say I live a life free of any bipolar-related issues. My bad days are probably a bit worse than some, and my good days would exhaust many. I live each day knowing there's no guarantee that I won't end up back in the hospital. Those of us who share this disorder understand this all too well. What we get in return is the ability to experience life on levels some people never will.

A person diagnosed with bipolar disorder does not have to stop living. The best advice I can offer to anyone with bipolar disorder is to not let the disorder define you. Be aware of the symptoms that accompany mania and depression the same way a diabetic would monitor insulin levels. However do not dwell on feeling like you are "crazy." Everyone you know and or will meet in the future are "crazy" in their own way. A little piece of advice from having observed humans for the past twenty years, there is no such thing as "normal." People are funny and strange creatures. Never be afraid to let your freak flag fly. Just be aware of the illness you have and don't get to far off track. If you have a chemical imbalance that gets out of whack and needs monitoring. Get help from professionals who know what they are doing. Don't over think it. That is coming from someone who has already done enough of that for you...

It would mean a great deal to me if this story helps to chip away at this stigma. If one person reads this story and gains a new understanding of what manic depression/bipolar disorder is, then the late nights at the computer were worth it. Thanks for taking the time to read my story.

CLINICAL ASSESSMENT

By Michael Wall M.A., L.M.S.W.

Michael Wall M.A.., L.M.S.W., provides a brief clinical assessment of how Pete Barnes' story relates directly to the medical diagnosis of Bipolar I 296.04 Single Manic Episode with Psychotic Features as described in the *Diagnostic and Statistical Manual of Mental Disorders,* Fourth Edition Text Revision (DSM-IV-TR). The assessment offers psychology professionals precisely how the actions, thoughts, and feelings of a patient directly correspond with the current medical definition.

The following clinical assessment describes how Pete Barnes's behavior during the course of *Sixty Days to Sanity* relates to his clinical diagnosis.

It is rare to encounter a Manic Episode in an average weekly psychotherapeutic session. There may be tips (very individual to each person) that reveal a coming episode in someone already diagnosed. These include such things as sleeplessness, less constrained, unusual behavior, and confusion during which attention becomes scattered. This disorder (anecdotally) seems to be over-diagnosed currently in the United States. Too many cups of coffee and resultant intense anxiety—even over a period of hours—or episodic over-exuberance of personality does not equal a Manic Episode; this is a very serious and debilitating disorder with grave ramifications, and it must be taken seriously and with deference.

Peter Barnes was my patient in psychotherapy in the fall of 2007. At the time, he had come to see me for a common bout of anxiety, episodic to his current life situation. After a few sessions, we had talked through the issues and we were able to terminate his therapy. It is important to note that while Pete holds a diagnosis of Bipolar I, at the time of our meeting and since then, he has presented with no symptoms of Bipolar Disorder. He did communicate with very slightly pressured speech, though I believe this would have been indiscernible to a lay person who was not looking for symptoms of anxiety or illness. After hearing of and reading his account of the Manic Episode. my diagnosis for Pete is Bipolar I Disorder, Single Manic Episode Severe with Psychotic features, 296.04, which concurs with the determination of his psychiatrist. Any clinician in the United States diagnoses patients with the *Diagnostic and Statistical Manual of Mental Disorders* (DSM-IV-TR), and should necessarily come to this same conclusion given the same information. Here are some of the important facts listed in the DSM-IV-TR that occurred to me in reviewing Pete's story:

Pete was extremely goal-directed (a symptom of Bipolar Disorder) in finding the "rugger huggers," and in joining the radio station, and in various other situations. He continually interrupted his peers (at rugby meeting) to assert himself as his thoughts had achieved greater importance for him than the points of his peers. He described himself as a "motor mouth," which is a symptom caused by a "flight of ideas" during which the brain works faster than the tongue. Pete had an unusual need to have himself heard—and pressed the issue.

Holding up the line for the copy machine as he was obsessively working was a result of goal-directedness—not simply obnoxious behavior towards others around him, or social detachment due to a personality disorder, but because of his overwhelming need to achieve what he perceived as his goal for the moment.

Then, in Chapter 2, when Pete feels he is rising out of his bed and floating around, he is having what is clinically described as "depersonalization." This is not necessarily a symptom of Bipolar Disorder, but it is an indication that mental stress is occurring. A brief and lesser degree of this (feeling estranged from one's body or self) is not uncommon, and occurs in half of adults sometime during their life, usually precipitated by severe stress. In hindsight, we can now consider the onset of mania the severe stress that caused Pete to feel the way that he did.

Pete states he "no longer had any time for any of my friends" because his tunnel vision kicked in. "I wanted to walk faster, talk faster . . . no one could keep up with me."

His statement that "My mood turned a 180 degrees in second" is a clinical indication of unstable mood called labile affect. When he left the radio station meeting after yelling obscenities to silence the room, this action did not give him pause. At the station, he described how his radio show would change the world. This demonstrates two possible Bipolar Disorder symptoms: grandiosity and delusional thoughts. A delusional thought is one that is not held by others and is insupportable by reasonable logic and is an indication of psychosis.

Pete was going to put the school radio station on the map in a week. He was certainly "goal directed," while at the same time easily distractible. Earlier, Pete had read all of the numbers on the pressures and temperatures of the earth's core and was ready to make a transmitter to broadcast his thoughts telepathically. This is another delusional belief.

His assertion that "My thoughts would flow faster than I could write" is again a flight of ideas.

The statement "I tried to read the thoughts of passersby" represents delusional thinking that can be involved in a number of other different disorders, but is a definite clue that there is mental imbalance.

At one point in the text, Pete says, "The Wright brothers had nothing on me." This was another point of grandiosity as he inferred that he was greater than those with international acclaim. The running and hitchhiking flight down the turnpike was manic in nature and demonstrated unreasonably enthusiastic behavior.

As Pete stated, "My new brainchild involved constructing a transmitter strong enough to broadcast from the center of the earth. I could simply transmit my radio show telepathically to the box, and then the box could relay my message to every person on the planet." This is a good example of delusional thinking that is psychotic and that necessitates the "with psychotic features" part of his diagnosis.

Pete's realization of a deep-rooted parallel and his struggle to understand mania (in relation to his friend Damian's) depression corresponds with the DSM-IV-TR point that the two poles of mania and depression share an equal level of intensity.

The Differential Diagnosis: (What this may look like, but it is not)

First of all, it is clear that this is not Schizophrenia as there were delusions but no hallucinations: or grossly disorganized speech or behavior, negative symptoms or catatonia.

Something to note is that one can be diagnosed with Bipolar I Disorder by experiencing a Manic Episode with no hint of depression. This is the case with Pete's episode.

Many times there are other diagnoses that the symptoms might resemble. A clinician needs to "differentiate this disorder from

263

other disorders that have similar characteristics (DSM-IV-TR)." The Manic episode in Bipolar I Disorder must be distinguished from episodes of a Mood Disorder Due to a General Medical Condition or a Substance-Induced Mood Disorder. Further, "Bipolar I Disorder can be distinguished from Major Depressive Disorder and Dysthymic Disorder by the lifetime history of at least one Manic or Mixed Episode. Bipolar I Disorder is distinguished from Bipolar II Disorder by the presence of one or more Manic or Mixed Episodes rather than a Hypomanic (manic of less intensity) Episode. This disorder should also not be confused with Cyclothymic Disorder, Psychotic Disorders, and Bipolar Disorder Not Otherwise Specified. (DSM-IV-TR)."

A clinician must make sure that the symptoms do not indicate Schizophreniform Disorder, Schizophrenia, Schizoaffective Disorder, Psychotic Disorder Not Otherwise Specified or Delusional Disorder. Many Disorders, like personalities, overlap greatly, so therefore, a diagnostic decision should never be rushed. The important thing is to assess people as individuals with sometimes complex behaviors, rather than as a group of symptoms to categorize quickly for an insurance company or for any other important purpose.

<u>Diagnosis</u>

In satisfying criterion A of Bipolar I Disorder, Pete had a persistently elevated mood lasting one week.

Pete clearly demonstrated all seven symptoms, when only three are required to satisfy criterion B of a Manic Episode in the DSM-IV-TR.

Furthermore, the symptoms did not meet criteria for a Mixed Episode (Criteria C), and the mood disturbance was severe enough to cause a definite lapse in occupational functioning or in usual social activities or relationships with others, or to necessitate hospitalization to prevent harm to self or others, and there were psychotic features (Criteria D) (DSM-IV-TR). Finally, in relation to criteria E, the symptoms were not caused by a chemical substance.

The point to my section of this book is that while there were clear symptoms of Bipolar I Disorder, Pete has now lived 20 plus comfortable years after being diagnosed. He has adhered to his medication prescription, does not drink alcohol and lives as a happy functional adult. It is now clear that others can do the same.

RESOURCES

Below are descriptions and web addresses for the national organizations that act as the primary resource for people with any form of manic depression. These organizations are dedicated to reducing stigma and creating resources to make the lives of those who suffer better.

Internet technology has made it easy to find support groups and confidentially research the options for you or friends and family dealing with this disorder. On these sites you can: locate information about medication, find books, share stories, become an advocate and much more. There are so many people ready to help, please use what is out there.

Active Minds - www.activeminds.com

Active Minds is the only organization working to utilize the student voice to change the conversation about mental health on college campuses. By developing and supporting chapters of a student-run mental health awareness, education, and advocacy group on campuses, the organization works to increase students' awareness of mental health issues, provide

266

information and resources regarding mental health and mental illness, encourage students to seek help as soon as it is needed, and serve as liaison between students and the mental health community.

NAMI – National Alliance for the Mentally Ill – www.nami.org

Colonial Place Three, 2107 Wilson Blvd., Suite 300, Arlington, VA 22201

Phone: 703-524-7600; NAMI HelpLine: 1-800-950-NAMI

The National Alliance for the Mentally Ill (NAMI) is a nonprofit, grassroots, self-help, support and advocacy organization of consumers, families, and friends of people with severe mental illnesses, such as schizophrenia, major depression, bipolar disorder, obsessive-compulsive disorder, and anxiety disorders.

Depression and Bipolar Support Alliance www.ndmda.org

730 N. Franklin Street, Suite 501, Chicago, Illinois 60610-7204 USA

(800) 826-3632 (312) 642-0049: fax (312) 642-7243

Nationwide, DBSA chapters offer nearly 1000 peer-run support groups where you will find comfort and direction in a confidential and supportive setting, and where you can make a difference in the lives of others. Most groups are volunteer run and provide self-help through facilitated meetings.

Federation of Families for Children's Mental Health

www.ffcmh.org

1101 King St. Suite 420

Alexandria Virginia

Off:(703) 684-7710

A national parent-run non-profit organization focused on the needs of children and youth with emotional, behavioral or mental disorders and their families

uthor biography

The author has lived successfully with Bipolar Disorder since 1989.

Two years after being expelled and escorted off campus by security during his severe manic episode, Barnes was elected vice president of the student body at the same university. After graduating with honors he successfully pursued a career in television and radio advertising and completed six years of service to the Pennsylvania Army and National Guard. The author's passion for comedy inspired him to produce a year long comedy series in Snowmass, Colorado, featuring top stand-up comedians from across the country. A passionate athlete, he also competed in a triathlon, and he snowboards and mountain bikes for recreation.

A person suffering from mental illness who tackles life with such vigor gives a valuable perspective to patients and family members as they try to understand how to cope with Bipolar Disorder. By sharing the intimate details of this experience, Barnes hopes to chip away at the stigma associated with the condition.

MAY ALL YOUR

VISONS BE FANTASTIC

Made in the USA
Charleston, SC
26 May 2011